ALSO BY WAYNE JOHNSTON

The Mystery of Right and Wrong
First Snow, Last Light
The Son of a Certain Woman
A World Elsewhere
The Custodian of Paradise
The Navigator of New York
Baltimore's Mansion
The Colony of Unrequited Dreams
Human Amusements
The Divine Ryans
The Time of Their Lives
The Story of Bobby O'Malley

JENNIE'S BOY

A NEWFOUNDLAND CHILDHOOD

WAYNE JOHNSTON

Alfred A. Knopf Canada

Library and Archives Canada Cataloguing in Publication

Title: Jennie's boy : a Newfoundland childhood / Wayne Johnston.
Names: Johnston, Wayne, author.
Identifiers: Canadiana (print) 20220139482 | Canadiana (ebook) 20220139520 |
ISBN 9781039001664 (hardcover) | ISBN 9781039001671 (EPUB)
Subjects: LCSH: Johnston, Wayne. | LCSH: Johnston, Wayne—Childhood
and youth. | LCSH: Johnston, Wayne—Family. | LCSH: Goulds (N.L.)—
Biography. | CSH: Authors, Canadian (English)—Biography. |
LCGFT: Autobiographies.
Classification: LCC PS8569.O3918 Z46 2022 | DDC C813/.54—dc23

Text design: Terri Nimmo
Jacket design: Terri Nimmo
Image credits: Courtesy of the author

Printed in the United States of America

10 9 8 7 6 5 4 3 2 1

Penguin
Random House
KNOPF CANADA

For Jennie and Lucy

JENNIE'S
BOY

one

Jennie and Dad worked in town, where we had lived for a while, but we could not afford to live there anymore, so we were going back to where we came from with our tails between our legs.

My parents would have to go back to riding a yellow bus to work because two men had come and taken our car, which, because of something Dad had done, we couldn't afford anymore. The men had come in their own car, but one man got out and climbed into our car, and then they drove both cars off while the neighbours watched from the windows of the house across the street. A shameful sight that Jennie said no one would ever forget.

We were gathered in the kitchen just as we had gathered in many other kitchens before we'd had to leave a house for good because Dad had spent the rent. "I may as well tell you the truth straight out," Jennie said, as if she had managed to keep the truth from us until now, but she'd be damned if she would gild the lily yet again for a man like Dad.

Dad had spent the rent in some bar that was close to where we lived. It was bad enough that he'd spent the rent, Jennie said, but to do it right under our noses was an all-time low. We'd barely been in St. John's long enough to afford to get a phone installed, and we'd have to pay for it for the next month, but we wouldn't be there to hear it ring or use it to ring someone else. She hadn't even memorized the number yet.

Dad said it was just a phone, not a family heirloom. But then he admitted he was guilty for what the rest of us would soon have to endure because of him. We might as well convict him in advance. He was no good and never had been and never would be, he insisted, and his wife deserved a better husband, and his four boys a better father. He insisted on it as if he saw more clearly than Jennie ever could the disappointment to her that he was. Dad continued to expound on his utter worthlessness, as if he was giving someone else the dressing-down they long had coming to them until, at last, Jennie relented and told him he was being too hard on himself. Soon, they were both heaping contempt on some nebulous, sinister enemy who didn't know a good man when they saw one, some universal agency of opposition that was forever thwarting the modest plans of decent men like Art Johnston.

Dad said he would be shamefully on display throughout the journey tomorrow from St. John's back to the would-be hamlet we had abandoned just three months earlier. Our old neighbours would say that Art Johnston had found out the hard way that he was no better than anyone else in the place whose very name he so disliked that he refused to use it.

But then he went back to insisting that it was all his fault, and this time the four of us boys—Ken, Craig, me, and my little brother, Brian—joined Jennie in defending him from himself, contradicting him when he said we would never have a decent home as long as we were stuck with him.

"You're being too hard on yourself, honey," Jennie said, and the four of us said that she was right, that it wasn't his fault that the world was full of bad men who took advantage of the good, that there was no lower you could go than to be a landlord who cared about nothing but the rent. A landlord was a man who lorded it over others.

Dad shifted sides again and told us of the landlords he had known, heartless men who turned families out on the street in the middle of winter. He had been under the thumb of dozens of them, he said, but never ceased to be amazed by their ruthlessness and trickery. But the day was coming, he promised us, a better day, when nothing we owned would be seized by landlords because we couldn't pay the rent.

"That day might be just around the corner," Jennie said, and we all nodded and huddled around Dad and told him you never knew when good times were coming, when your luck was bound to change. It wasn't as if he had it easy. Raising four boys was hard enough, but when one of those boys was more trouble than the other three combined, it might as well be seven or eight that he was taking care of. He looked at me and I tried to smile.

"It's not Wayne's fault, either," Dad said. If truth be told, it was only because of bad luck that the deck was stacked against us, not because of him and me. Soon the others were all conceding that it wasn't my fault. It wasn't his fault. It wasn't the fault of his wife or the rest of his children. None of us could help how we were born.

Still, by this time, everyone was huddled around *me*, and I was crying and promising to do my best with what I had. I couldn't be blamed for all the things that were wrong with me, nor could Jennie, any more than Jennie's mother could be blamed for having a daughter who'd had a boy like me.

I was seven that November when we were tossed from our apartment in St. John's. I had lived in twenty houses by then. I don't remember a lot of them, but most of them were scattered along a couple of roads in a place called the Goulds, about an hour away from town. It wasn't much of a place, not even a village, but it was where Jennie was born and where her parents, Lucy and Ned, still lived, on Petty Harbour Road.

On that last night in town, Jennie said she remembered all the houses. She said she could give you directions to the bathroom in almost any house on Petty Harbour Road. It wasn't much to brag about, but it was true.

We boys never knew when we were leaving or exactly where we were moving next, just that we were always one car breakdown or appliance repair away from having an eviction notice slipped beneath our door in the middle of the night by a landlord who, Dad said, was too gutless to look him in the eye.

"Too gutless," Craig said.

"We don't always have a car," Dad said, "but we always have Wayne, and there's no telling when he'll have to be repaired."

Repairing me seemed to be impossible because no one seemed to know why I was sick. A doctor I could not remember having been to see had once said I had a nervous cough. Jennie seemed to think I had a nervous cough because I was nervous all the time. She said she had heard of other people who had nervous coughs, but she never named them.

Calling it a nervous cough made it sound like I was constantly trying to clear my throat, but that wasn't the case. The cough was so deep, so loud and so relentless that each of my three brothers had tried to kill me to shut me up.

Once Ken had shoved a half-used bar of soap into my mouth when he was trying to get to sleep. Soon, though I was no longer coughing and Ken was drifting off, I was frothing soap bubbles. I don't know which of my brothers alerted my parents but, when they saw me, they took me to be having a seizure. They were distressed but not especially surprised, as they had, by this time, all but reconciled themselves to the idea that I would not make it out of childhood. They called a nurse named Dot Chafe, who lived nearby. She had seen seizures before and knew I was not having one. Exploring my mouth with a pair of tweezers, she was able to remove what was left of the soap.

Another time, I was sharing the back seat of one of our family cars with Craig when the door swung open as my father turned to go up an especially steep hill. Craig pushed and kicked me from the car and watched through the back windshield as I tumbled down the hill until I came up against a mailbox, miraculously unhurt but for skinned knees and elbows. Craig said he'd done it not just to spare himself my endless hacking but to see what me flying down the hill would look like.

And Brian once pinned me to the kitchen floor and jammed a plastic egg cup into my mouth so hard Dad couldn't pry it loose. He had to crush it between his thumb and forefinger so that Jennie was able to pick the pieces from my mouth.

Sometimes Jennie spoke as if everything else that was wrong with me followed from my cough, but other times it seemed to be the other way around—I coughed because I had no appetite and was therefore sickly and had no energy, things you would think would incline me to sleep a lot, and yet I almost never slept. Ever since I could remember, I had always been generally, vaguely *sick* and, as far as anyone could tell, I always would be, for however long I could endure it.

No one ever spoke in front of me about how much longer I would last, though when Dad set eyes on me after having been away for a couple of weeks inspecting fish plants along the coast, he often said, "Talk about beating the odds." That I had survived, even to the degree I had, astonished him.

Jennie had several times come close to miscarrying me. When I was three, an emergency appendectomy had nearly done me in, as had a routine tonsillectomy when I was five, and several bouts of pneumonia. And there were all my chronic conditions—throwing up whatever I managed to get down, the nervous cough, the insomnia. A man in the Goulds named Luke Joyce had beaten the odds by being born the seventh son of a seventh son, and yet, Dad said, I had beaten greater odds by not having perished. It was Luke Joyce, not a doctor, that Jennie once called when I was sick to ask him to say a prayer on my behalf. She credited Luke with having saved me, even though the next time she called him, my condition got so much worse she never called him again.

When Dad criticized her for such superstitions, Jennie always countered that you only had to look at the number of people who died in hospitals to know that they were the last place a sick person should go. Dad told her that this was irrational— more people would die if not for hospitals, just as they did in the places around the Bay that had no hospitals. He'd seen with his own eyes the harm that superstition and lack of education could do.

Dad was proud of being an educated man. Born into a fishing family, he had left Newfoundland, earned a diploma in agriculture and come back and found a job as a lab technologist with, of all things, the federal department of *fisheries*, sometimes travelling the island with a small group of other men on a laboratory boat, testing the quality of fish processed in the fish plants in remote coastal settlements. He told us he had seen poverty and ignorance on a scale that would have made Dickens despair of doing justice to them with pen and paper.

He had once happened upon a woman who had had twenty-one children by Caesarean section. Jennie said that this woman sounded like a kangaroo from one of the rum dreams he was forever waking from. Dad swore that the woman had a scar on her belly that looked like a big zipper. Jennie mumbled something about the big zipper and the little zipper and asked him how he knew what her scar looked like. Dad said because she liked to show it off. It was the closest thing to a conversation piece the God-forsaken town would ever have.

Jennie said she bet the woman was a piece, all right, but doubted that what she was famous for inspiring was conversation. And she cited the case of a woman they both knew who went into hospital for a minor operation on one ear and came home deaf in both.

Dad became exasperated. Why would hospitals even exist if they did more harm than good? He didn't know of anyone else who thought they did the very thing they were invented to prevent.

She said you only had to ask around to find out that more people agreed with her than agreed with him.

Yes, he said, because most people were ignorant, superstitious and uneducated, which was exactly what he had started out saying in the first place. Parts of the world would forever be backward until their people came to understand the value of scientific thought.

Jennie reminded him that he was not a scientist and he was not a doctor. All he did was work for the fisheries department. The next time she tripped over a sick fish, she'd be sure to bring it straight to him.

two

It was cold in the back of my grandfather's stake-bodied truck. Crouched down, we boys huddled against the cab that blocked the wind, staring in through the window at the backs of the heads of Ned, Jennie and Dad, Jennie so short we could barely see her, the tail of her nylon scarf between the shoulders of the two men, who themselves were very short, especially Dad.

Jennie was two months pregnant. Her mother, Lucy, said that you'd think she'd already be showing, a woman her size. That she wasn't showing had Lucy wondering if Jennie's new baby would be the size I was when I was born—a full-term baby of three pounds.

Dad did not like my grandmother, blaming her for Jennie's superstitions. Lucy did not like Dad. I once asked her how tall Dad was. Who knew how tall he would be, she said, if you took away that tidal wave of hair and Brylcreem that you couldn't budge with a baseball bat. "He should never wear a suit and hat. They make him look like a boy dressed up as a man for Halloween. It's not his fault. It's not Jennie's fault that she's so short. It's not my fault that she was so small when she was born. It's not my fault that when she was a youngster, she gave up eating for Lent and forgot to start again. Anyway, your parents are a good match. Like salt and pepper shakers. They might not stand out among the dishes on a dinner table, but you're glad they're there when the food is really bad."

Before we'd moved to town, I'd spent whole days with my grandmother after I was sent home from school by Sister Paschal, the principal of St. Kevin's, who said that parents didn't want their kids sitting in a classroom with a child who was forever coughing from what, for all they knew, was tuberculosis, but even if it wasn't, it was surely contagious, and if it wasn't contagious it was so distracting as to make it hard for any of them to concentrate. Then, when we'd moved to St. John's, she'd called the principal at my new school to recommend that I stay home come September, too. By now I hadn't attended school in six months.

I could tell there was no talking going on in the cab of the truck because the three of them kept staring straight ahead. Jennie was likely dying for a smoke, but it was unthinkable that she would smoke in front of her father, let alone in his truck.

Jennie had charged my brothers with the mission of making sure I didn't catch my death. So Craig held my jacket closed at the throat with one hand and kept my hat from blowing off with the other, and Ken and Brian pressed against me to shield me from the wind. Still, November was not the worst month for switching houses. That, we all agreed, had been March of the year before, when it took us two hours to go from our old house to our next one, half a mile up the road, because of a snowstorm. We overshot the driveway six times before we found it by accident. Every now and then, I looked up at Craig's round, fierce face, red from the cold, his nose running, his hands red, too, though he blew on them from time to time and tried to stretch his too-small stocking cap down over his ears. He had a cold sore—it seemed he was never without one—that he kept dabbing with the back of his hand to see if it was bleeding.

Ken wasn't wearing a cap or gloves, and his jacket and shirt were open at the neck, but he didn't seem to care. He was four-teen and had been wearing glasses since he was five, ones with thick lenses and thick frames. This pair was held together at the corners with white adhesive tape, and Jennie had added a piece of elastic that tied at the back of his head to keep the glasses from falling off. It left a permanent dent in his hair.

Brian had his face pressed against the glass and his hand on his cap to keep it from blowing off. I thought of one of the rare times when Jennie let Dad buy us ice-cold bottles of Coke. Brian had guzzled his, and the sheer pleasure of it had brought tears to his eyes. He was five but bigger than me and bigger than most five-year-olds.

His world was the six of us. He loved each of us fiercely and fearlessly. He once rammed his head into the stomach of a huge man who was trying to pick a fight with Dad. The man was so amused by Brian's ferocity that he picked him up by the armpits and held him in the air above his head while Brian flailed about, tears running down his cheeks, then put him down and walked away.

Brian felt what we felt. He cried when one of us cried. He took all of our sides when we argued with each other, and begged us to stop arguing. He looked out for me, his smaller, older, sickly brother.

We drove west, my brothers, my parents and me, all of us facing the way we were headed, as if we were keeping our eyes peeled for a house, as if we had our pick of all the houses we were passing and so far had deemed none of them acceptable, none that looked like we would be able to make a go of it there and never have to move again.

Even in a city so small it barely deserved to be called one, there had been noises and smells that made me forget the woods we were returning to.

I looked at the wind-bent junipers of the Goulds, the dark spruce trees, the fields in which house-high rolls of hay would spend the winter, all of it glistening because of a mist that wasn't far from snow. I heard the cries of the small birds, which, in St. John's, had been drowned out by the screeching of the seagulls that had never in their lives pitched in a tree. I wouldn't miss the brake blasts of trucks and buses that made their way downhill from one stop sign to another, nor any of the other noises I had listened to in town as I lay awake all night, every night, while the others slept.

I glanced at Ken and fancied that his glasses made everything look different and that he didn't really see the woods. Maybe he was staring into the future, to the high school back in town that he'd be going to next year. There was no high school in the Goulds. For grades nine to eleven, Catholic boys were bused to a school in St. John's called Brother Rice and the girls to Holy Heart. Ken rarely complained or wished for things we couldn't have. Whatever he saw through his glasses reassured him, and his quiet, untroubled manner reassured me.

Craig couldn't pretend that things didn't bother him or that things would be better in the future. He couldn't say to himself, "Never mind." He knew that, unlike Ken, he might not make it out of the Goulds. He was wary of everything he saw and everything he was told and everything that, if he fell for it, might hold him back—like a girlfriend he would have to marry when he was still in school, like sticking up for those who might not deserve it because they might not back him up when the kind of people who never stuck up for anyone in their lives started handing out the blame. That made me his biggest problem, because there was no one he felt more obligated to protect who was less able to protect himself than me.

Craig stood to see where we were, squinting as he looked out over the top of the cab, one hand on his cap, the other on mine. "Ruby Line," he said and crouched back down again. He moved his hand to my shoulder. "Are you cold?"

Teeth chattering, I shook my head, and he laughed.

"We'll get there soon, unless we're headed somewhere farther up the Shore this time."

I hoped the truck would slow down and listened for the sound of the turn signal—I didn't want to live up the Shore, where no one would know us unless we went all the way to Ferryland, where Dad was born—and there, we'd have to live with Dad's brother and his wife and kids, as we once had to do for three weeks, the six of us sleeping on the floor of their front room.

I looked in through the window of the cab. With so much time in a small space with his always silent father-in-law, Dad was likely dying for a beer. He'd been on his best behaviour, not drinking, acting as if he'd never had a drink in his life. I knew that, for a while, he would continue to wear a shirt around the house instead of going bare-chested, which he did when he was drinking. He would comb his hair in an especially high wave and keep it in place with even more Brylcreem than usual. He wouldn't say a word unless Jennie asked him a question. He wouldn't tell us to be good no matter what we did. He would jingle the change in the pockets of his pants as if he didn't have the slightest doubt that this time his new leaf would last and didn't mind that the rest of us were certain it wouldn't.

At last I heard the clicking of the signal and saw that we were turning left. "Petty Harbour Road," Craig announced. "We better not be staying with Lucy and Ned again."

"We better not," I said, and he rolled his eyes, knowing I wouldn't mind at all if we stayed with Ned and Lucy.

"We're slowing down right beside their friggin' house," he said. But we didn't turn left into Lucy's yard. We turned right, into the driveway of the place across the road.

We all stood in the truck bed and stared at the house, one I'd often looked at from the window of Lucy's front room. It hadn't been lived in for years, though it was newly painted, and the lawn had been mowed, as had the little ridge of turf that had grown down the middle of the driveway. A token effort to spruce it up.

"No friggin' way am I living here," Craig said.

"Maybe we're just parking," Ken said, and Craig rolled his eyes again, his expression bitter. No matter what he said or did, he would have to abide by a decision that people less savvy than him had made on his behalf.

I knew that this house was cheaper than the one we'd left in town—the house we moved to after we'd been evicted always was. We'd likely stay just until Jennie found something better, as she somehow always did, maybe a house we had already lived in and been evicted from before.

We all climbed out of Ned's truck, and Ned backed out of the driveway. His hands in his pockets, Craig ambled toward the house in a way that said that he had moved too many times to be suckered into thinking that this place would be any better than the others. But the rest of us, even Ken, ran to see the inside, hoping there were things to be discovered, like oddly shaped nooks and crannies or items the previous tenants had left behind.

Even the houses I did remember, I didn't remember all that well. I'd so often been sick, flat on my back on the rollaway cot we called my bedmobile, half attending to the sound of the TV, to the music, to the voices of the characters and those of my parents and my brothers, half-lost in a kind of semi-sleep, a dream whose content was somewhat determined by whatever ailment, or combination of ailments, I was contending with. All the houses seemed to have become one: old, small, rundown, drafty, with a roof that leaked.

The most unusual thing about this house was that the landlord had walled off the stairs to the upper storey, probably,

Dad said, because of the state of the sagging saddle roof. So it was really a very small one-storey house, with two bedrooms, a bathroom, a kitchen with a tiny adjoining dining room and a front room. Dad, Ned and a few of my uncles had already moved in what little furniture we had left.

Craig appraised the fridge and stove and declared them to be second-hand, saying the words in a way that implied an extreme degree of second-handedness. To Craig, second-hand meant that something had been used until it was useless.

As I followed Craig about, he said in a low voice that Dad didn't know how to fix anything and only made things worse by trying, recalling the time Dad had once blown his thumb-nail off while trying to fix a radio that, because he'd been drinking, he'd forgotten to unplug.

Craig said Dad always let himself be cheated when something had to be replaced or fixed. There had been a steady stream of repairmen through the houses that we lived in, and whatever they repaired soon broke down again. Dad, who had searched the classifieds for the cheapest handymen, denounced them as hacks when they turned out to be as inept as their self-descriptions in the ads should have led him to expect. When the fixed appliance broke down again, he went into a paroxysm of scorn, saying the repairman didn't know how cats were fixed.

"You don't get what you pay for," Jennie always said, "you get what you *can* pay for."

Dad appraised the house as if he'd never set foot in the place before. He regarded the second-hand fridge and stove, the washer and dryer with the skepticism of a man who had so often been taken for what little he had that he had come to expect it as much as everyone who knew him did.

Nothing passed through more hands before it wound up in our dad's than a television set. The sight of a TV repairman lugging his suitcase-like kit of tools and tubes from his van to our house so filled Dad with dread that he would go to bed until the man had left. He and Jennie had lain awake in bed one night, smoking cigarettes, while she tried to convince him it was not his fault that we now had a TV with an upside down picture tube, or that we had to turn it upside down to watch it, its four legs sticking out at angles until Dad removed them and Jennie put a lamp on it that made it look even more absurd.

"This takes the cake," he said now, looking around at the unopened boxes on the floor.

"Never mind about it, sweetheart," Jennie said, but Dad began to hold forth about being trapped in a life wholly unlike the one he had imagined for himself. Yahoo after yahoo, he said. As fast as Hibbs Hole could turn them out, they wound up on his doorstep. Word had spread far and wide that there was a chump on Petty Harbour Road who would fall for any scam, just waiting to be had. The name Art Johnston would soon be a synonym for gullibility. Many of these backward, inbred nitwit repairmen would soon wind up in our living room, wearing lab coats, *lab coats* for Christ's sake, just like his own. And why not? How unlike them was he, a mere technologist, a cartoon scientist who fell for these pitchmen whose credentials were no phonier than his? What did he do all day that was so much grander than what they did? He looked through a microscope and counted bacteria, which was just a fancy way of saying that he counted—he *counted*. He did what he was taught to do when he was five.

The more he tore himself down, the sadder the house became. I went into the bedroom that would become my brothers'. Ken was already lying on the bare mattress of the upper bunk of one of two bunkbeds with his glasses on, as if, though it was not time for bed, he despaired of ever getting to sleep. Craig lay on the lower mattress, facing the wall, eyes wide open, while Brian, on the lower bunk opposite, looked as desolate as I felt.

"Craig," I whispered, "can I sleep in here tonight? I won't cough, I promise."

"No," Craig said. "All you ever do when you lie down is cough. Wheel your bedmobile out to the living room and close the door behind you."

"But it's only six thirty."

"I don't care."

It had been a common sight for years, me pushing my bed about on its wheels, leaning my head and shoulders into it, one or more of my brothers pitching in to help when the bed began to swivel from side to side. Even when I wasn't sure how sick I was or would soon be, I preferred sitting propped up in my bed to sitting in a chair, because there was no telling when a coughing fit would force me to lie down, even though lying down sometimes made it worse. I usually reclined at a forty-five-degree angle and got about two fitful hours of sleep per night, less or none when my cough was worse. Craig, who thought it was impossible to get as little sleep as I did, insisted I must be faking it. He crept out of his bed many times in the hope of catching me napping, only to find me wide-eyed and waiting for him.

And Jennie, too, had had insomnia since she was a child. Even as a preschooler I couldn't sleep, and Jennie would sit with me, working on jigsaw or crossword puzzles, neither of us dozing more than one or two hours a night.

"I don't know why I don't sleep," she once said. "I don't know how other people do it, stay in one place for so long in the dark."

I was about to wheel the bedmobile out of the bunk room when Dad appeared in the doorway and said we should have a housewarming party, just for us. He announced this as if it was a new idea, though we had a housewarming party just for us whenever we moved. A new home, he said now, is a reason to celebrate on a Friday night. As my brothers scrambled from their beds, Dad said to hold on—that Jennie was cooking something in the kitchen, and she would tell us when to join them there.

To pass the time until she called us, Ken and Craig had me crawl inside my folded-up bed, my head sticking out one side, my feet out the other, and they pushed me about the house as fast as they could, zigzagging around pieces of furniture.

I didn't mind, though I felt giddy and queasy and my feet and head sometimes banged against things, provoking Jennie to yell that it would be their fault if they broke the bed or I got hurt.

Ken and Craig spun the bed about, one of them holding my head, the other holding my feet. It wasn't long before I was warning them that I would get sick if they didn't stop, but they kept on spinning me, laughing, trying to see how fast they could whirl me and how long I could stand it before I started crying.

"One of these days," Jennie said, poking her head out of the kitchen, "he's going to go flying out of that bed, straight out the window, and there'll be no one laughing then."

At that my brothers stopped spinning the bed and slowly and carefully extracted me from it, easing me out as if I might break or throw up if they weren't careful.

Jennie at last called out to us. She had made a batch of dough for toutons and was now frying fistfuls on the stove. We hadn't had toutons since the last time we moved.

When they were brown all over, she piled them on a plate in the middle of the kitchen table. We sliced the toutons partway in half, crammed their insides with butter that melted instantly, then jam and cream, and washed it all down with steaming cups of tea.

I ate as much as I could, praying that I didn't bring it all back up, then watched with envy as my brothers carried on gorging themselves.

Jennie and Dad didn't eat any. Jennie's appetite was the size of mine, but somehow she was never tired, never sick. It was as if her body was sustained by the cigarettes she smoked. She reeked of Rothmans. So did Dad, though a lot of his cigarettes burned away in the ashtray because he forgot about them once he got going on something after he had had a drink.

When the toutons were finished, my brothers went to bed, but I stayed up with Dad and Jennie, as they knew I would.

"Another palace," Jennie said, looking around.

"Another palace," Dad said, raising his glass as if she'd made a toast. Since he was still on his best behaviour, he wouldn't drink too much tonight, and Jennie kept him company, nursing her own Royal Reserve whisky and ginger with ice. "The Winter Palace, like in Russia." He smiled as he always did when he made an obscure allusion and didn't explain it, and Jennie nodded faintly.

Dad got going on the name of the Goulds, which was where we were now and the place where most of the houses we had lived in were still located, now lived in by others. No one knew why it was called the Goulds, he said. It wasn't the name of anyone who lived in the Goulds, or *had* lived there, or anyone he had ever heard of who lived anywhere else, but what made it even worse as a name was putting "the" in front of it.

Not many places were called "the" something. There was the Bronx, but that was the name of a *part* of a place, a part of New York City, and it was just a nickname anyway that no one knew the meaning of. He said that if we were going to call where we lived "the" something, it should be something that made sense. The Goulds was little more than a clearing in the woods, he said, so better that we call it the Woods.

Jennie said he had bigger things to worry about than why the Goulds didn't have a better name. She said that we didn't live in the woods. We weren't wild animals, and we couldn't go around calling the place something different than everyone else.

Dad said that everyone should call it whatever they felt like calling it.

What sense would it make if everyone called the same town a different name, Jennie said. Imagine the confusion. The whole point of naming *anything* was to avoid confusion. There were three hundred people in the Goulds—

Dad interrupted, saying there were people in the Goulds odd enough to inspire three hundred nicknames.

Jennie ignored him and said imagine if each person in the Goulds had three hundred names. You'd never know who anyone was talking about.

Dad said that was good because it would make gossiping impossible.

Jennie said she could see how that would suit *him*, but it would leave everyone else with a lot of time on their hands.

Dad said he was sticking with the Woods, at least when he was talking to his boys.

Jennie said that she better not hear him or us referring to the Goulds as the Woods.

In that case, Dad said, he wouldn't call it anything. He'd think of euphemisms for it.

Like what? she said.

He said he would have to give it some thought. He said the Goulds was not a real name because it didn't mean anything.

Jennie said that he was from Ferryland but no ferries had ever gone anywhere near Ferryland, so what did Ferryland mean?

He said he didn't know, but at least "ferry" and "land" were words, and people had been living there for three hundred and fifty years before anyone lived in the Goulds.

Jennie said so what if Ferryland was a lot older than the Goulds. It *looked* a lot older. Younger was better. When he was older, he'd wish that he was younger. Everybody did. Every place started out as a place where no one was born. Every place started out without a name. She said that Ferryland was like an old man whose hair had fallen out. It was old and bald, just as he would be someday.

He said that the Goulds sounded too close to the Ghouls, which was hardly a selling point. On the other hand, no one would be lining up to live in the Goulds no matter what it was called. But wasn't she embarrassed when people thought she said she lived in the Ghouls? He said the reason it didn't have a proper name was that it wasn't really a place. No one was in charge of it. There was no mayor or council. It wasn't incorporated. There was no sign that welcomed you to the Goulds, nor one that thanked you for visiting. No one knew or seemed to care where the Goulds began and where it ended. It was just a stretch of unpaved road between Kilbride and Bay Bulls, with houses strung along it. A region, an area, like the ocean or the woods or the hills, only smaller, a road flanked by farms like my grandfather's, small farms that dated back to when the woods were cleared partway up steep hills that allowed views of the ocean when the weather was just right, which wasn't often. The Goulds could not be found on even the most detailed map of Newfoundland. The road was sprayed with oil in the summer to keep the dust down, and all but unmaintained the rest of the year.

As he'd begun to say before she interrupted him, he went on, if it was going to be called the *something*, it should be something that meant something, like the Sahara or the Milky Way.

If he wanted a different reaction when he told people where he lived, Jennie said, she was pretty sure that telling them he lived in the Milky Way would do the trick.

She got going on Ferryland again. The only trees left there weren't really trees because they were half his size and wouldn't grow another inch, and that was saying something. Nevergrowing evergreens. She said that being near the ocean had stunted their growth just as it had stunted his. If he had grown up away from the ocean, among the real trees of the Goulds, he might now be closing in on five foot three.

He said the trees were shorter than *her*, too, and that was *really* saying something.

She said she was so short because her mother, Lucy, had had a hard time while she carried her. "I can't tell you how many times you were written off," Lucy had told her. The doctors told Lucy it was pointless to hold out for a child who'd wind up killing both of them. It was suicide. But she was tough. She told them they didn't know for sure. Maybe her baby would make it but not her. Or the other way around. Or maybe neither of them or maybe both of them. There was only one way to be sure, and she thought it was worth the risk. They said Jennie would be born premature, but she wasn't. They said they'd have to cut her out, but they were wrong again.

"That was why I ignored the doctors while I carried Wayne,"

Jennie said. "I can't tell you how many times *he* was written off, either."

Dad said he knew how many times. It wasn't as if he wasn't there. If he knew how to count how many bacteria there were in a morsel of fish, he knew how to count how many close calls his son had had, but he had to admit that the day might come, if I didn't perish first, that my close calls would outnumber the bacteria in even the lowest grade of fish.

Jennie said he shouldn't talk about me perishing in front of me as if, on top of everything else, I was deaf. Dad said, talk about someone who had already inspired three hundred nicknames.

She grabbed the flask of Royal Reserve and screwed the cap back on, then put the flask in the cupboard and gathered up the glasses and dishes on the table, leaving only Dad's glass in front of him. "This housewarming party is over," she said.

"I was just joking," Dad said. He looked at me. "I didn't hurt your feelings, *did* I?"

I shook my head. I didn't want the party to be over. I didn't want to sit up by myself any longer than I had to on my first night in this strange house.

Jennie leaned back against the sink and crossed her arms and looked at him as if she was daring him to say another word. Did he want to know the nicknames people had made up for him?

He got up from the table, went to the bedroom and eased the door shut. I knew that when he shut it like that, he wanted her to join him.

"Don't mind your dad," she said. She crossed the floor to me and took me in her arms and kissed the top of my head.

Then she went into the bedroom, from behind the closed door of which a radio began to play country music. Jim Reeves. Kitty Wells. Patsy Cline, who went out walking after midnight.

Within a week, the house was as close to furnished as it would ever be. There was a Formica kitchen table with six padded chairs from which the stuffing stuck out through the canvas covers, so Jennie taped them up.

In my parents' bedroom, there was a double bed and two lamps on night tables. In the bunk room, the two double bunk-beds. In the tiny dining room, there was a table that I quickly made my school desk. In the front room, there was a chester-field and two badly chipped coffee tables that Jennie varnished several times. She bought cheap gauze curtains and plastic blinds for all the windows.

The whole house smelled of mothballs, a problem she didn't bother addressing because, she said, it wouldn't be long before the whole house smelled of cigarette smoke.

"By the time you're finished, we'll be moving out," Dad said one night. "We can't take a cent of what you're spending with us."

But she bought and covered the walls with floral-patterned paper in spite of Dad's protest. "It's our *home*," Jennie said. "That's how we should think of it no matter how long we might be here."

He said she had wallpapered half the houses in the Goulds, put new linoleum on half the kitchen floors, new curtains on half the windows. She was a one-woman renovation squad who worked for free. By sprucing up a rented house, all she did was make it possible for the landlord to charge the next tenants more than he charged us.

She said she doubted that it was possible to spend more money sprucing up a house than he spent sprucing up the man who owned the nearby tavern called the Crystal Palace, a man who must have celebrated when he heard that Art Johnston was moving back from St. John's.

Then they went to bed and played the radio again.

For the next couple of nights, I lay on my bed and watched TV with the others or parked the bed in the kitchen and merely listened as they played cards.

I stood the bedmobile against the wall in the bunk room when I wasn't using it. I sometimes slept, or tried to, in the bunk room, where there was technically a bunk for me, but as soon as I started coughing, Ken and Craig lifted me and my bedmobile out to the living room. Even when I wasn't coughing, the rasping, rattling sound of my breathing forbade sleep for all of us.

I was likewise banished from the living room when the others were watching TV and my coughing was especially bad, making a return trip in my bed to the bunk room, where the noises I made were of less nuisance to the others, though Jennie often sat on one of the bunks beside my bed, attending to me, nervously watching over me even as she smoked a cigarette that worsened my condition.

three

By all rights, Jennie should have been as sickly as me. She chain-smoked and ate next to nothing because of chronic heartburn. She was now forty, and her esophagus was a tube of scar tissue. She had taken to declaring herself unable to stand another bite after forcing down her favourite meal, a boiled chicken wing and two slices of tomato. She weighed seventy-five pounds and stood four foot ten—a tiny woman who had given birth to each of us, even me, without any sort of pain relief, deeming all women who resorted to such things to be crybabies. Minutes after having each of us, she phoned Dad to tell him she was ready to come home.

She was a stenographer who changed jobs almost as frequently as we changed houses, often getting fired before she began to show when her boss somehow found out or guessed that she was pregnant. But there were so many stenographer jobs available that, while still pregnant with the same child, she was sometimes able to get another one—she was fired three times while carrying Craig.

Two weeks after we moved back to the Goulds, she was still home with me. I was supposed to go to Lucy's, but Lucy couldn't take me because she had some sort of a condition that acted up from time to time, and it was acting up now.

I had been missing Lucy. The first thing I remembered her ever saying to me, when I was maybe four, was "When you meet your Maker, ask Him why he did such a piss-poor job with you." To help me grow, she fed me cod-liver oil that came in yellow plastic bubbles. "I don't know why I bother," she would say. "It won't do you any good even if you drink a jug of it."

While we were waiting for Lucy's health to improve, Dad had been taking the bus to work in town. The whole situation was fraught with peril in more ways than one—staying home with me was costing Jennie money, and there was no telling when, instead of coming home on the bus, Dad would go to a bar.

At night, I watched the open door of my parents' bedroom from the bedmobile in the living room. The glow of Jennie's cigarette in the darkness came and went like a lighthouse light. One morning, after worrying about everything all night, Jennie told Dad he would have to go back to cutting hair on weekends to make up for the wages she was losing.

"Christ," Dad said.

There was no barber in the Goulds, so, years ago, Dad had bought a basic barber's kit to cut his sons' hair. Word got around, and soon Art Johnston was in the weekend haircutting business. He charged only twenty-five cents. Jennie had made him give it up when he started spending every quarter he made at the Crystal. This time, she said, he was to give the money straight to her.

Soon, in what we had begun to call the half house, there were boys I'd never met sitting on a chair in the middle of the kitchen while Dad sheared them nearly bald, often nicking their scalps because he'd had a few drinks whose smell he tried to disguise with aftershave. Rows of disconsolate boys, shivering in the November cold, sat against the back of the house, waiting for their turn to have their hair removed so that they could go around for the next few weeks looking like undersized Marines. The ones who came to Dad were always the poorest boys, and the Johnston haircut advertised their poverty to everyone.

One of Dad's customers was John Longhoffer, the most immaculately dressed and smoothly complected of all the foster boys who came to St. Kevin's by way of Fleming's Home for Wayward Boys, as Lucy called it, in honour of that local family's reliance on the income from taking in such children. John had famously ruined his new school blazer in a dust-up in which he held his own against the gym teacher and Sister Paschal, after which he was merely suspended, as he was a few months later for unzipping his fly in class to prove that he had pubic hair to a boy who wouldn't take his word for it. There had been a time when, as fellow outcasts, we had been something like friends, but then I'd had to leave school. When he took his spot on the chair in front of Dad in our kitchen, I said hi, but he pretended not to notice. I had become someone that even John Longhoffer didn't want people to think was his friend.

"Well," Jennie said at dinnertime near the end of November, "as of tomorrow, Wayne is going to be spending as much time at Lucy's as he does here."

Dad sniffed but said nothing.

The next morning, Craig helped me wheel the bedmobile across the road and into Lucy's porch, then lit out for school. I pushed it past the door, which Lucy had left open for me, as had always been her habit. I found her in the kitchen, sitting at the large, round wooden table that she and Ned had been given by their children as a twenty-fifth anniversary present, a cup of tea in front of her.

"There he is with his contraption," she said. "You're like the sick in the Bible who carry their pallets around with them."

She got up and crossed the kitchen floor, put her hands on my shoulders and looked down at me.

"Do I look like I've been sick?" she said.

She didn't, so I shook my head.

"You look like you *are* sick," she said. "Mind you, if you didn't, I'd think there was something wrong with you."

Lucy's eyes were as dark as burnt raisins. Her eyebrows were almost as dark, but her hair was white and had been since she was forty, mid-length and curled under at the sides. She wore a wine-coloured housecoat-length cardigan, unbuttoned, over a beige, wrinkled dress that hung down almost to her slippers.

We began the day as we had each day I had ever spent at her house, with her making me a glass of Quik. She spooned the chocolate powder into a glass, filled it partway with water and put ice cubes in it.

I drank without pausing to breathe while she watched with wonder. Ice-cold Quik was the only thing I was always able to keep down, though it was sometimes a struggle. Jennie never bought it, saying it was too expensive.

"Stop," Lucy said after I'd had about three gulps. She took the glass from me, put it in the fridge and put a saucer on top. She would ration it out to me, three gulps at a time, for the rest of the day. It was the only thing she would serve me, because I could never manage lunch.

"There must be something very special in Quik if someone as picky as you can stomach it," Lucy said. "Still, at that wedding feast in the Bible where Christ changes the water into wine when they run out, He wouldn't have made much of an impression if He'd gone round spooning Quik into everybody's glass, even though it would have been a miracle because there *was* no Quik back then. A miracle per se is not enough. It has to be something good. If all He'd known how to perform were miracles that made things worse, He would have been hard put to find twelve apostles for the Last Supper. That's a sin for me."

She crossed herself, bowed her head and mumbled a prayer, then said, "So, what's the news from home?"

I told her what Dad and Jennie talked about during the housewarming party. She said they shouldn't make fun of the house. Maybe it wasn't a palace, she said, but it would do until our palace became available, which might be a while because of the long waiting list for palaces in Newfoundland.

I told her Dad had said something about a winter palace in Russia and asked where Russia was. She said she was fairly certain that Russia's location was the same as it had been since my father read about it in some book. It was probably farther from Newfoundland than Nova Scotia, which was as far from home as my father had ever been.

Unable to think of any other way to stand up for Dad, I reminded her that he spoke Latin. She said not unless he had picked it up from palling around with priests, which was unlikely because Father McGettigan had been trying and failing for years to find someone to go bowling with. "Your father remembers bits and pieces of Latin that he learned in school from teachers who remembered bits and pieces of Latin that *they* learned in school. That chain goes all the way back to when, for some reason, *everyone* spoke Latin."

She didn't know why priests had to learn Latin, but she was glad they weren't singing the Mass in Latin anymore, because it made for a nice change to understand what they were saying, even though they *sang* just as badly in English as they had in Latin. She said that Christ would have suffered more if, instead of making Him endure the crucifixion, God had made Him listen to Father McGettigan singing about it. She crossed herself.

"Seven years to become a priest—you'd think the Church could spare one year for singing lessons." She crossed herself again and bowed her head and mumbled another prayer.

I asked her if she confessed to Father McGettigan the things she said that were so sinful she felt she had to cross herself.

"I'd be in the confession box day and night if I did," she said. "McGettigan wouldn't understand anyway. He never starts off a sermon with 'Have you heard the one about . . . ?' It's better for me to tell God on the spot that I'm sorry for what I say. Not that Christ was in the habit of making jokes that cracked up the apostles." She crossed herself.

After the Quik came my bath, which she gave me while I was standing up—the proper way to bathe a child, she said, though Jennie had once said it was just a holdover from the days when Lucy had bathed her own children in a washtub in the freezing porch.

As she poured jugs of soapy water over my head, telling me to keep my eyes tightly closed, she did a running critique of my emaciation.

She enclosed my wrist with the circle of her thumb and forefinger. "See, I'm not even touching you," she said, "that's how skinny you are."

I told her she had warned me to keep my eyes closed, so how was I supposed to see?

"Your mother must have tried to pay for you with expired

coupons and had to give half of you back. You're so skinny I can see your soul."

I asked her what it looked like.

"It's even paler than the rest of you. Not a mark on it except from original sin. Like a scuff mark from a boot. Like your forehead on Ash Wednesday. Except the mark of original sin wouldn't come off if you used all the Javex in the world."

"Is that true?"

"Keep your mouth closed or you'll die from too much soap. You were three pounds when you were born. You must have had lungs in you the size of sardine gills. A good-sized drop of rain would have drowned you."

She poured another jug of water over my head. She said that if she poked me in the back her finger would come out through my belly button. She poked me in the back and said, "Don't look! It's an awful thing to see, my finger sticking out of your stomach."

"No, it's not," I said, but I didn't look.

"They left you a fine scar when they took out your appendix. They must have pulled you apart with their bare hands. What's an appendix for, anyway?"

"You told me to keep my mouth closed."

"Close it after you tell me what an appendix is for."

"I don't know," I said.

"They took out your tonsils, too. What are they for?"

"I don't know that, either."

"You had appendicitis and you had an appendectomy. You had tonsillitis and you had a tonsillectomy. First comes the *itis* and then comes the *ectomy*."

"I've had bronchitis about ten times," I said, "but they never took anything out."

"Then you must need your bronk for something, but I don't know what it is. They tell me that I have pancreatitis. They tell me it gives you gallstones or something. I've already had my gallbladder out. That was some kind of ectomy, too. The word was about a mile long. I'll go to the hospital one of these days and come home without my pancreas, you mark my words. Another ectomy. Not that I know what a pancreas is for. Your father's haircuts are ectomies too. There's youngsters going round the Goulds with half their heads missing."

"That's not true."

"What are we going to do with you, Wayne? Your spine sticks out like a string of peppermint knobs. Your breastbone, too. Your collarbone looks like a coat hanger."

I wondered what the options were when it came to what to do with me. Still, I felt as strongly as anyone else that something had to be done with me.

"Your knees are like ankle bones," she said, "and your ankle bones are like thumb knuckles. You have the boniest little arse. You'd have saddle sores if you had to sit on a chair for more than an hour."

When she was done bathing me, she dried me with a towel, saying that now I'd had a proper bath instead of one sitting in water that was grey with my own dirt. Then she carefully brushed my hair and sprinkled my cheeks, holy-water fashion, with cologne she said Ned hadn't touched since someone gave it to him for Christmas twenty years ago.

"The clothes you came across the road in will have to do,"

she said, "though I could make better myself than what Jennie can afford to buy you."

When I was dressed, she declared me to be as close to presentable as she could make me for what always followed my bath.

"Let's go in and we'll light a candle," she said.

To "go in" meant to go to the room known as Lucy's Shrine. It had once been the bedroom of two of her five sons, who had slept in the same double bed until one of them, Leonard, died of tuberculosis when he was seven. The other, Dennis, did not get sick at all.

There was a single bed in the room now, and a large oval rug, worn from age to the point that only a faint trace of its floral pattern remained. As always, the curtains were drawn, creating the kind of half light there was in church on cloudy afternoons. Where the headboard of the larger bed had been, the wallpaper was still less faded, though it was thirty years since Leonard had died.

To the right of the bed was a small round table on which there was a three-foot statue that towered over me: the Blessed Virgin Mary in her robes of blue and white, eyes modestly downcast, her right hand raised in benediction, the Baby Jesus in her other arm, a crown on His little head. In front of the statue was an unlit votive candle in a jar made of frosted blue glass, like the ones that you could light in church after you put a donation in a metal box on the wall and said a prayer of intercession for mercy on the soul of someone who had died. In front of the candle were framed photographs of relatives Lucy had lost, not just Leonard.

We knelt side by side in front of the statue and blessed our-selves.

"Light the candle," Lucy said, handing me a box of Sea Dog wooden matches. I lit a match, then held the flame to the wick of the candle until it caught. Lucy took the lit match from me, blew it out and put it back in the matchbox, which she took from me and tucked in the pocket of her sweater.

"Now we'll say a prayer for Leonard," she said. Silently, I knew she meant. We folded our hands and bowed our heads. I was so intent on watching her out of the corner of my eye, I didn't even say the Hail Mary, let alone a prayer for Leonard. When she blessed herself again, I did, too.

"Mom and Dad," she said, pointing to one of the photos, as if I'd never seen it before. A couple about her age stared, unsmiling, at the camera.

"That was taken in front of the first barn your grandfather built. They went with Ned and me on our honeymoon to Har-bour Grace. Dad slept in a room with Ned, and Mom slept in a room with me. They thought hotels were wicked places and didn't want their daughter seen in one with a man the strang-ers of Harbour Grace might think was not her husband.

"That's my sister, Helen, there. She became a nun. She was at St. Kevin's for a while, but no one who knew her when she was growing up would take her seriously as a nun, so she had to go someplace where no one ever heard of her.

"And there's Eileen. She married a man from Boston. She's only ten in that picture. She was so down-to-earth until she met her husband. After that, you had to make an appointment to kiss her arse." She sighed. "I'm speaking ill of the dead. You're not allowed to do that even if what you say is true." She blessed herself, waited a few seconds, and did it again.

Then she pointed at the only photograph of Leonard known to exist. Taken in one of the hayfields, it showed him with Ned, who was sharpening a scythe. Leonard was grinning at the camera, wearing a baseball cap, or something like one, sideways.

"You know you're the spitting image of Leonard," Lucy said for the umpteenth time.

It was a resemblance that did not endear me to my grandfather but, rather, reminded him of his life's greatest loss. Leonard, Lucy said, had been not so much Ned's favourite as the only thing in his life that never rubbed him the wrong way.

I looked at that picture of Leonard. It terrified me that I was the spitting image of a boy who looked like that, a boy who had died because he looked like that, a boy who had perished from sheer Leonardness.

I was Leonard in the flesh, inasmuch as there was any on my bones. Leonard, though smiling, was hollow-eyed and already tubercular. I didn't think I looked like him. I didn't think I looked tubercular. The only thing my mother remembered about Leonard was seeing a doctor pull a white sheet over his face.

"Leonard dying turned Ned as sour as pickle juice on everything," Lucy said.

"He still likes *you*."

"He knows who cooks his food."

Was that it—was Ned afraid to love anyone lest he lose them and suffer again the pain of losing Leonard? I didn't want to remind anyone of someone who was dead, especially not a boy my age or close to it.

"What's it like in heaven?" I said, knowing that Lucy wanted me to ask.

"Heaven is perfect. My little boy has been there a long time. He needs me."

Leonard, she believed, was still seven years old, still sick, alone in heaven with no one to keep him company. He had been up there all this time in that perfect place yet remained exactly as he had been when he died. Her still little, ever-dying boy had been keeping watch for her, looking out a window in heaven, waiting for her to arrive, fretting that she never would. He missed her even more than she missed him. The idea tormented her. And yet she believed that heaven was perfect.

Since Lucy first told me this, I hadn't been able to get the vision of him, staring out of a window in heaven, out of my head. What a grim vigil to be keeping in such a supposedly perfect place.

"If you go before I do," Lucy said, "I'll put a picture of you here and light a candle and say a prayer for you every day."

I wanted to ask her not to talk about me going, before her, with her or after her. Instead, I said, "Why do you have to pray for someone who's already in heaven?"

"You ask God to have mercy on their soul."

"But they're in heaven. Why do you have to ask God to stop picking on their souls?"

I wanted to tell her that she was confusing heaven with purgatory, or glossing over purgatory, or something.

"God is some strict," I said instead.

"God loves everyone," Lucy said.

"The souls in purgatory burn for millions of years, and the souls in hell burn forever," I said. "I wouldn't set fire to someone I loved. I wouldn't set fire to Dad because he spent the rent. I wouldn't set fire to Craig because he stole seven cents from the pocket of Dad's pants like he did last week. I wouldn't think it was fair if someone sets fire to me for pretending I'm sicker than I really am."

"Have you ever done that?" Lucy said.

"Maybe," I said. "Just a little bit."

"Have you confessed it to the priest? I know all the tricks when it comes to confession. Don't confess made-up sins that the priest will go easy on you for. That would be a real sin and you'd have to confess it sooner or later. Imagine confessing that you made up a phony confession. After that, no matter what you confessed, the priest wouldn't believe you. 'Bless me, father, I have sinned. You can't believe a word I say. Even that might not be true. I might have made that up.' I don't think it's a good idea to confuse a priest. He might give you the wrong Penance. Imagine if the doctor gave you the wrong prescription."

"What would happen?"

"Nothing. You might as well chew a stick of gum as take a pill. Since you look like someone rolled out a batch of dough and draped it on a scarecrow, there's no harm in preparing yourself for heaven by making a good confession. You shouldn't put it off. God won't give you three weeks' notice. He won't give you one cent of severance pay."

I started to cry.

She pulled me to her and kissed me on the head. "Don't mind me," she said. "The only way you'll go before your time is if I scare you to death. Don't you worry. I'll be in heaven with Leonard when you get there."

Next, we played crazy eights. She always tried to let me win, but I never did. She said she had never known anyone to be so bad at cards. "Never mind," she said. "Everyone is good at something, even the ones that are good for nothing. I don't mean you."

We talked a lot as we played. She had a way of savouring the pronunciation of diseases as if they were her favourite foods, sometimes lingering so long over a syllable that it became two, such as the last one in pneumonia. *Pneu-mon-i-a. Tu-berc-u-lo-a-sis.*

"Where's Murchie?" I said, growing bored with cards.

"Where he always is," Lucy said.

Murchie was a former barn cat that Lucy had turned into a house cat. Murchie was short for Murcheson, a name Lucy had always liked but had never been able to persuade Ned to give to one of their sons.

In the hope of seeing the cat, or even enticing him out to play, I went over to the daybed and got down on my hands and knees and lifted the edge of the blanket that draped it.

Lucy warned me not to get too close because the cat would scratch my eyes out.

I saw Murchie's yellow eyes, glowing in the dark, intent on mine, though he kept to the corner where the two walls met, the floor all around him covered in grey cat hair.

We'd never had a pet. Not only were they forbidden in some of the places we rented, but Jennie had also made it clear that we'd never have a pet until we had a house of our own. A dog or a cat would just be a nuisance to a family that moved so often, just one more thing she would have to take care of.

Even as cats go, Murchie was indolent, spending most of the time sleeping in the sunlit parts of the house, moving sluggishly from room to room until there were no patches of light left, then sliding like a snake beneath the daybed, only emerging now and then to visit his food dish or homemade cat box, which were in the porch. Lazy and chubby though he was, Lucy said he was good company for her, what with how silent and self-absorbed Ned was and how often he was out in the fields or in the barn.

"I can see him in there," I said. "He might come out if I offered him a treat."

"I told you, he'll scratch your eyes out," Lucy said. "There's still a lot of barn cat in him."

"Really?"

I thought of the half a dozen scrawny cats whose job it was to catch and eat mice in the barn before the mice ate or spoiled the grain and hay. Ned had no time for anything that didn't pull its own weight or serve some useful purpose around the place.

"Yes, really. When I took a shine to him, I coaxed him out of the barn by feeding him scraps from the house. Small trout. The oil from cans of sardines. The juice and fat from baked beans—he loves them. Barn cats kill one another sooner or later, or something else kills them, so I asked Ned if I could make Murchie a house cat. I had to nag him for a while. Eventually, he said that Murchie had better not get under his feet. I had to wean Murchie off the outdoors. It was almost two years before he would eat what I put down for him and use the cat box instead of mewling to be let out day and night."

I let the edge of the blanket fall back into place and rejoined Lucy at the table. "Does Murchie like you?" I asked.

She said that, like Ned, he knew where his food was coming from.

But did he like her?

She said she doubted it. When I asked why, she said there was no point asking why when it came to cats.

Sometimes we discussed how little my grandfather talked. Lucy had her theories.

Flanking the many cart roads on the farm were heaping rows of large fieldstones, washed to a dull grey by the rain that had fallen on them since Ned had single-handedly pried and dug them from the ground and carried them to where they were now. Miles of lichen-coated rock walls divided his farm from the ones on either side of it and divided his own land into sections in which he grew different crops. In one field that was too wet and soggy to be cultivated lay the weather-whitened stumps of all the trees Ned had pulled up by their roots so that the forest could make way for the farm.

Lucy told me it took Ned four years to clear something you could call a farm from the steep hill on which it lay, and then he needed to maintain the entire farm by himself until the first of his sons was old enough to join him. "Four years of spending your days with no one to talk to but a horse might do a lot of damage to your gift for gab," Lucy said, "assuming you had one in the first place. And who's to say he did? I know men who are too shy to talk to themselves."

At noon Ned came in from the fields for lunch. Exactly at noon. Under his outer clothes, he wore what Lucy called his farm uniform—coveralls, a checkered shirt over a white under-shirt, and heavy grey socks. Still feeling bloated from three gulps of Quik, I sat through lunch with her and Ned, watching them eat their cold cuts and tea buns in silence. I could hear every sound the house made, especially the furnace cutting in and out.

The only other sounds were of clinking cutlery and of Ned drinking his tea. He poured some on his saucer, then raised the saucer to his mouth and blew on the tea to cool it and then loudly slurped. It was all I could do to keep from laughing. Lucy's eyes reminded me to pretend I hadn't noticed and not to say a word. That was easy to do because Ned *never* spoke to me. He didn't exactly ignore me. He didn't pretend I wasn't there. I could *feel* him noticing me. He simply didn't speak to me. "Don't feel special," Lucy told me once. "He never speaks to anyone. He may not talk your ear off, but I think someone talked both of his off before we met, because he doesn't seem to hear a word even when *he* says it."

Throughout lunch, he and Lucy did communicate now and then. Did he want a second helping? He nodded his head. Did he want a third? He shook his head. Was he going to nap on the daybed after lunch? He nodded again. That meant that Lucy and I would have to sit in the living room in total silence until he went back to work in the fields.

Did he want the last of the tea? He nodded. Lucy poured it for him. He added milk and sugar, then poured some onto his saucer.

At that point Murchie stuck his head out from beneath the daybed, the blanket draped around him like some sort of shawl. Then he came all the way out, his tail twitching. Crouching, as if he thought that none of us could see him, he began to inch toward the table, his big yellow eyes fixed on Ned, his ears perked at the sounds Ned made drinking his tea. "Bwwwphhhh," he blew, then slurped. "Kshleeup."

Murchie crept a few inches, then stopped, crept a few more, then stopped, his gaze never wavering. I looked at Lucy, who, buttering a tea bun, seemed oblivious.

When the cat was about halfway to the table, Lucy turned ever so slowly and looked at him. He looked back at her, unblinking. As if she had made her point, she looked away.

The next time he went to move, she stopped him by sternly saying his name.

"Murchessssson."

It was like a hiss. The hair rose on Murchie's neck and back.

"*Murchesssson.*"

He kept his eyes on Ned.

She loudly stamped her foot.

Murchie turned and, faster than I would have thought possible, even for a cat, he bolted beneath the daybed. Ned, absorbed in his saucer of tea, continued to stare straight ahead.

Then Ned took his nap on the daybed, his head on the pillow just inches from where Murchie lurked below. The instant Ned woke, he went back to work.

Lucy sat at the kitchen table and sighed, one hand on her cheek, the other on her chest. "Murcheson's been doing that every day for weeks," she said. "I don't know what's got into him. That man and that cat are going to give me a heart attack."

"Murchie stopped when you stamped your foot."

"I told you—he knows where his food is coming from. And he likely knows where he'd end up if he went aboard of Ned— back to the barn. But what if, some day, he doesn't stop?"

"I don't think Ned is afraid of him."

"Maybe not. But he should be."

"Maybe Murchie just wants a taste of tea."

"What he wants a taste of is Ned's upper lip."

"He never slinked out like that when I was here before we moved to town. Maybe he missed *me*."

"You were missed, but not by Murcheson."

I asked her if cats went to heaven. "I never heard of a cat going to heaven. Or hell or anywhere else. In the Bible, pets

47

are not exactly front and centre. Maybe some animals were pets before they were sacrificed. Jesus didn't have pets. Jesus was all business. There's nothing in the Bible about Him wandering around with a dog named Rover and teaching him to fetch a stick. That's a sin for me." She crossed herself.

"I don't know about cats. I haven't got it all figured out. There were plagues of frogs that caused warts. I wouldn't want a pet frog that could give me warts. It's not like frogs have a lot going for them in the first place. Add warts into the mix and you'd have a hard time taking a shine to one. There were plagues of locusts back then, too. You'd have to be awful stuck for a pet to try to make one out of a locust. You wouldn't get a lot of affection back from one. You'd have to keep it in a little box, I suppose. How would you tell it apart from all the others if it got loose? It wouldn't come when you called it. How would it know its name? And what would you call a pet locust?" She fell silent, pondering, then said, "Animals might have their own heaven, I suppose, some place where they'd be safe from us and safe from each other. Everyone getting along. I don't know where animals go when they die. Going nowhere is not much of a reward for being slaughtered, roasted and eaten, is it?"

four

About a week later, at the end of the day, Lucy and I knelt on the chesterfield in her front room and watched the road, waiting for the yellow bus that would drop my parents off at six o'clock. My heart sank when I saw Jennie step down from the bus alone.

Lucy said it was a shameful thing that everyone on the bus had seen that Jennie had come home from work by herself, all the way from St. John's to the Goulds. Now she had to walk up the driveway to the front door, as conspicuously alone as she had been on the bus, a pregnant woman on a bus by herself, disgracefully unaccompanied by her husband, who, as everyone on the bus well knew, was sitting in some bar somewhere in town, drinking beer among strangers, paying three times what it would have cost at a corner store.

"She'll rip into him for that when he comes home, whenever

that will be," Lucy said. "There won't be a cent of the rent left."
And then the word would go round about that, too.

That evening, as we did on all such evenings when Dad didn't
come home, the five of us ate supper in silence. My brothers
and I stayed at the table in solidarity with Jennie while she did
the dishes and afterward stared blankly at the ashtray in front
of her. We didn't budge until she told us to go watch TV.

We were all in the boys' room, me in my bed between the
two bunks, none of us asleep, when Dad came home. We
heard him stumble up the front steps, the door opening, him
declaiming he was sorry, that he had only intended to have
one or two drinks until he happened upon a friend whom he
hadn't seen in ages. Then we heard Jennie whispering urgently
that he had to go to bed.

Being told to go to bed didn't mean that Dad was getting off
scot-free, only that his comeuppance was being deferred till
he was sober, till they were next alone in the house or somewhere else or maybe right in front of us, depending on her
mood and how much of the rent he had spent.

I hated it when she ripped into him. I hated those words,
ripped into him. They might rip into each other. There was no
telling what people would do or say when they were ripping in.
Everything would go out of control, as it did when I coughed
so hard I couldn't catch my breath. After they were done, it
would seem impossible that they would ever speak again, and

the prospect of that, the idea that everything would be forever spoiled, would set me to coughing, which would make them rip into each other even harder.

Jennie waited until after they got off the bus the next day and he was following her down the driveway to the house. I was standing with Lucy in the open front door of *her* house, where Jennie had stationed us as further chastisement to Dad.

"You might as well steal the food right off your youngsters' plates," we heard Jennie say. "You might as well tear the clothes right off their backs. They'll wind up begging in the streets because of you. We all will. Not you, maybe, but the five of us. You'd probably spend whatever we could scrounge up—I wouldn't put it past you."

"Go home," Lucy said then. "Tell Craig to come get your bed."

Jennie was still at it an hour later, after ordering all of us boys to stay put in the bunk room. I began to cough and to feel as if I would be sick. Craig rubbed my back in circles while Ken lay on his bunk, staring at the ceiling, his hands behind his head. In the bunk above the one that was always empty, Brian pressed his face into his pillow, his hands clasped around it as if he was trying to smother himself.

There was a racket in my head like there was when I had a fever. I felt as if someone was rattling a can full of marbles right beside my ear. A voice that seemed like it couldn't be

Jennie's said words that ripped into me, and I felt the guilt that Dad was feeling and the sense of being cornered, with no choice but to cover up and take it.

I began to sweat so much my shirt got wet and then my hair. The room seemed to shake like a hundred people were jumping up and down in the kitchen.

I heard Dad say again that he'd just been having a good time with an old friend, and Jennie said he was a liar who, if he thought there was any money in it, would sell off his young-sters one by one. "You'll put us in the poor house."

Poor house. Poor little house. Poor thing. The house that was so mistreated, so misfortunate, so neglected and univer-sally pitied that it was known as the poor house. I felt sorry for the walls, the beds, the ceiling. I wished there was some-thing I could do for the poor house, which had done nothing to deserve being ripped into.

Dad told Jennie he agreed with her. If ever a woman was right about deserving better, about her youngsters deserving better, it was her. If truth be told, he was worse than even she could do justice to in words, because there were no words for what he was and she shouldn't waste her breath telling him that *he* was wrong. He was no good, never had been, never would be, not as a husband or a father or a breadwinner. As for the boys, she would do a better job raising them alone than she would with his help and he would not have her debase her-self by speaking out in his defence, because where Art Johnston was concerned, you couldn't go too far, not even if you hired Shakespeare to denounce him on your behalf . . .

Dad kept going like this until the only way for her to dis-
agree with him was to tell him that he was a better man than
either of them gave him credit for.

She said he drank because no one could live up to the
expectations he had for himself. He'd set the bar so high he
had no hope of reaching it. If the worst thing you could say
about a man was that he drank because he tried too hard,
because he cared too much and was racked with guilt because
he could not tolerate his limitations—if that was the worst
you could say about Art Johnston, then let whoever wanted to
say it say it, but she'd be damned if *she* would stoop so low.

The only good thing about her ripping into him was that
it always ended with him humbly and silently accepting this
view of himself as a man who could not possibly attain the
heights of virtue upon which his eyes were forever fixed.

The ripping in was over. We went out to the kitchen. And,
as often happened after Jennie finished with him, Dad began
telling stories about his childhood in Ferryland.

Once, he said, when his family gathered to say the rosary in
the kitchen, each of them kneeling and resting their forearms
on a chair, his father did not put out his cigarette but simply
set his ashtray on the seat and kept smoking, even when it
was his turn to say the first halves of the Our Father and the
Hail Mary.

"Art!" Jennie said, fighting back a grin. "That's a lie and
you know it."

Dad said it wasn't a lie. He said that, from that day on, his
father had smoked during the rosary, and the children, if they

wanted to, had eaten apples. I thought about children saying the rosary with their mouths full of loudly crunching apples while their father puffed his way through it, pausing now and then to light one up. We all laughed, even Jennie, though she put her hand over her mouth.

As they could not afford hair cream, Dad went on, he and his father and brothers resorted to running their hands through sheep's wool until they had enough oil to keep their hair in place. Every male in the family, like every other male in every other family in Ferryland, took Confession and Communion and went on dates reeking of sheep, who, he said, if we took the trouble to look it up, were a source of the lanolin that was an ingredient of most hair cream.

We knew that the part about the lanolin was true, having looked it up before, but the more we protested the implausibility of the rest of the story, the more he feigned indignation at being ganged up on.

He told us of a pet crow his family had had whose tongue was split like a parrot's and who repeated things, especially inappropriate things, that the family said, such as when the priest came to visit and the crow would not stop repeating, "Father Noble is an arsehole. Father Noble is an arsehole."

He said that there was a fellow nicknamed Smokey, known not to be right in the head, who lived all his life with his parents. About once a year, he gave in to his compulsion to smoke a neighbour out of their house, stealthily climbing up onto their roof just after dark and stuffing their chimney with blankets, then remaining up there until the occupants and the smoke began to pour out through the doors and windows. At which point Smokey, in some strange declaration of triumph or satisfaction, would remove all his clothes before attempting a getaway. Smokey was always foiled and returned unharmed to his parents until, eventually, he was taken to an institution in St. John's, where he remained for the rest of his life.

Dad was never closer to being happy than when he provoked us into saying that not a word he uttered about Ferryland was true. We provoked him as much as he provoked us until everyone but him was laughing.

Earnest, straight-faced, pretending that we were offending both him and Ferryland with our disbelief, he went on riffing about his childhood until I saw by his eyes that, in the real Ferryland, in his real childhood, he *had* been happy as he never had been since and never would be again, that he wished that he had never left the place, never gotten older and been drawn into chasing after what, in the grown-up, modern world, the world of cities, careers, competition, disappointment, nepotism and betrayal, was thought to be important. He had no business living anywhere but in that town beside the sea, no business pursuing any sort of life but the one that he'd been born to, impossible though it was for him to return to it, impossible for so many reasons, us foremost among them.

five

It was a requirement of Jennie's that we say the rosary every night after supper in the kitchen. After the ripping in, a week of rosaries went by as usual, all of us kneeling on the floor, each leaning on a chair. Dad always did so under protest, which he expressed either with an ironic sigh or a roll of the eyes or by saying something to the effect that he was not going to beg a non-existent God to go easy on his non-existent soul in a non-existent afterlife. And Jennie always reacted by telling us that Dad was just joking, that it was because he was so scared stiff of God that he pretended to disbelieve in His existence. Besides, she said, praying was not begging.

Dad said it sounded like begging to him. *Pray for us sinners. Lead us not into temptation. Have mercy.* With a sigh that said he knew as well as she did that there was no chance that he would not relent, she waited for him to kneel at his chair, which he did at last.

There was something so sad and solemn about saying the rosary in the failing light of evening, the interruption into my life of an awareness of something nebulous but terrifying, limiting, ultimate, something that would prevail over all else no matter what I did.

More than once, during the rosary that week, I fell into a coughing fit so bad I had to be excused and sent to the bunk room, where Jennie closed the door behind me.

When it was Dad's turn to lead, he either recited so fast that it sounded like gibberish or assumed a tone of irony and a faint imitation of Father McGettigan's high-pitched voice until Jennie shot him a look.

Then came one of the times we *all* dreaded.

On the last night of November, there was a lightning storm that was especially severe. I was awake on the bedmobile in the living room, reading *Tom Sawyer* by the light of a single lamp, when Jennie came running out of the bedroom in her pajamas, shouting as if she was still in the middle of a nightmare. "Come on, come on, into the kitchen now, *now*."

I heard Dad call out from his bed that he was staying put. Before she could tell me to, I joined Jennie in running about the house, drawing all the curtains closed, turning off whatever lights were on, unplugging whatever was plugged in, exhorting my brothers to find their prayer beads, go to the kitchen and kneel down. I was her partner in panic.

As thunder crashed directly overhead, she screamed, "Merciful God," and put her hands over her ears.

"It's only a *storm*," Dad shouted. But Jennie ran every which way, calling for us at every flash of blue or crash of thunder until Ken, Craig and Brian came out of the bunk room and Dad from the bedroom and they all pitched in to storm-proof the house, Dad swearing every time he ripped a cord from the wall.

Then we gathered in the darkness of the kitchen, where, after Jennie lit a candle and put it on the table, we knelt and Jennie began the rosary. Brian and I were more upset by her terror than by the storm, Brian crying, me coughing.

"It's just a warm front moving in," Dad said when it came his turn to lead. "It's not the wrath of God." Then lightning flashed and deafening claps of thunder followed and Jennie covered her face with her hands and dropped her head onto her chair, crying and unable to take her turn. It went on like this until the worst of the storm had passed.

Dad helped Jennie to her feet and put his arms around her as she buried her head in the crook of his neck.

"Boys," Dad said, "plug everything back in and open the curtains."

We did as he said, none of us making eye contact. When we got back to the kitchen, Dad wasn't holding Jennie anymore and she'd stopped crying but was still wiping her eyes with the heels of her hands, smiling sheepishly.

As I knew he would because he always did, *he* ripped into

her: What good did she think it did to close the curtains? Did she think that the curtains kept us safe? Did she think every other family in the Goulds was doing this?

Maybe, she said.

Lightning and the Goulds had been around long before her, and the Goulds had managed to survive. Did she know of anyone in the Goulds being hurt by lightning?

She said no, but that didn't mean it hadn't happened.

He said, so they were *secretly* hit by lightning?

She said houses could be blown apart by lightning.

He said it was all over the Goulds in an hour if someone broke a window, but a family had somehow kept it a secret that their house had been blown apart by lightning? He said we were safe because we were indoors. The house was grounded. She didn't have to scare the living daylights out of the boys, especially Wayne, who, one of these nights, would cough up his lungs while the rest of us were busy saying prayers.

Jennie, her arms now tightly folded, said she couldn't help it. Dad said that was because she didn't understand what thunder and lightning were. God wasn't playing target practice with lightning bolts, and Satan wasn't pounding on a giant set of drums. She didn't need to run around the house like a madwoman, waking everybody up, as if she just heard on TV that the world would end unless every one of the Johnstons got out of bed.

Jennie again said she couldn't help it, sounding more chastised than he did when she ripped into him. He said he was wasting his breath, because that woman across the road, her mother, Lucy, *Lucy*, had crammed her head with superstitious nonsense. Who in the name of God put up a statue of the Blessed Virgin in their house? In their *house*, for Christ's sake, where Wayne spent more time than he did in his own. No wonder Wayne had turned out as he had.

At that, Jennie finally began to fight back. He should leave Lucy out of it, because where would we be, where would *he* be, without Lucy, who didn't charge a cent for taking care of Wayne while they were at work, not that he could take care of Wayne, because who could do that *and* pay off the mortgage of the Crystal Palace? If it wasn't for Lucy, we wouldn't even be able to afford the shack we had wound up in.

Thunder and lightning, he said, ignorance and superstition, magic, black magic, ghosts and Holy Ghosts and archangels the size of galaxies, wart- and cancer-curing Holy Water, all mixed up with fairies and witches and sprites and goblins, and toadstools, which, by the way, was another term for frog shit. This was what she inherited from Lucy. People rising from the dead. Three days dead and Christ comes back to life smelling and looking like he just got back from the barber and then took a bath before putting on a brand-new set of custom-fitting robes.

"Stop it!" Jennie said.

Dad said he was going back to bed before a rumble of distant thunder inspired her to have another go at the rosary.

After he was gone, Jennie lit a cigarette. "Go to bed, boys," she said. "He can't help himself, either, I suppose. It's hard to change how you were born."

∾

After we had finished supper a few nights later, when Jennie told us to get our prayer beads, Dad said that he was not going to say the rosary anymore.

"Don't be silly," she said, but Dad shook his head.

"Never again," he said, in a tone of defiance that he often used with her but was rarely able to sustain. "I've said it for the last time."

She promised him she wouldn't let herself be panicked by the next storm. When had she been known to break a promise? We would say the rosary once per night, period.

He shook his head and didn't make a show of looking her in the eye as he often did at the start of an argument he expected to lose. And he'd been drinking, the proof being that he was sitting at the table shirtless and in his bare feet, indifferent to making a good impression.

She said we couldn't have one person walking around the house while the rest of us were saying the rosary. He asked her why not. She said it would be disrespectful.

He said you could do things differently than other people and not be disrespectful of them.

She said that, if he didn't say the rosary, he couldn't watch TV while we said it because we would hear it in the kitchen.

He said he wouldn't watch TV.

Then what *would* he do?

Nothing.

Where?

He said he hadn't thought about it. Jennie said the rosary was something a family was supposed to do together. He couldn't just opt out of it the way he opted out of playing

Monopoly. It wasn't a pastime that one part of the family could pursue while the other part pursued another.

He said he wouldn't do anything to disturb us, but he had said the rosary for the last time. He got up from his chair, and she asked him where he was going. The living room. While we said the rosary? Why not? Because we would hear him in there. He wouldn't so much as smoke a cigarette, he said. But we would still *hear* him. Doing what? We'd hear him the way you *hear* a person, even if he just sits there. We'd hear him cough or clear his throat or shift about in his chair or whatever. He said that he would remain absolutely still and not say a word until the rosary was over.

But the rosary would be spoiled if the father of the family didn't say it, Jennie said. He countered that it wouldn't be spoiled for him, because it wasn't as close to being the highlight of his day as it was to being hers.

Jennie frowned. Fine, she said. But he couldn't spend rosary time anywhere that we could see or hear him, because it would be too distracting, too *odd*. He could go into the bedroom and close the door behind him and stay in there until we were finished.

He said that if he was going to be banished to the bedroom for an hour, he would have the occasional cigarette. She said we'd hear him strike the match and smell the smoke.

And that would spoil the rosary, too?

Why did he want to set himself apart from us?

He didn't, only when it came to the rosary, which we could join him in quitting and thereby reunite the family.

She said it was nothing to joke about and we were not about

to stop saying the rosary just because he had. What else was he planning to quit? Sunday Mass? Going to confession? Speaking of confession, was he going to confess to the priest that he had quit the family rosary? Maybe she would do that for him.

Fine, he said. Week after week, instead of confessing her own sins, she could make an argument to the priest that she deserved a better husband. She would never have to say Penance again, and the priest would assign him a double dose of it at least. She could use her confession time to tattle on him, and maybe that would catch on, maybe the priest would encourage it, because people were more likely to be honest about other people than they were to be honest about themselves. Maybe, from now on, confession would be reversed, and she would tell the priest about him and he would tell the priest about her and the priest could settle all their arguments or say who the winner was. He didn't care. She could do whatever she wanted because he was never going to say the rosary again.

That night, as we boys said the rosary, we kept sneaking peeks at Jennie, who looked admonished, defeated, embarrassed, but also, somehow, *seething*. None of us doubted that there would be a reckoning for this.

From the other side of the bedroom door, we heard a match being struck, and soon after there wafted out the smell of smoke. I imagined Dad in there, sitting on the bed, a cigarette in one hand and his ashtray in the other as he listened to us murmur in the kitchen.

"He's not saying the rosary?" Lucy said. "Not even kneeling for it? Why not?"

I shrugged.

"He should try saying the rosary alone with Ned. It's the only time the man ever says that many words in a row. The first word out of his mouth nearly frightens me to death. The rosary is a lot for just two people to say, especially when one of them is Ned. Every night he says the Our Father like it's something he just learned that afternoon. You never heard a man to stop and start so much. Tell your father I could use his help. What brand of pickle has he got up his arse now, anyway, I wonder?"

"He says the Bible is just fairy tales."

"I've heard that and worse before from people who change their minds pretty fast when something big goes wrong. You don't hear much talk about the Bible being fairy tales from someone on their deathbed. He'll find out what he really thinks about the Bible one of these days."

"He says there's no God."

She crossed herself, bowed her head and said a silent prayer, then crossed herself again.

"Murcheson has more sense than your father," she said.

six

Each night, after I had done the homework that Sister Paschal set for me, Jennie and I sat at the little dining room table that doubled as my desk and solved anagrams together. She had a book called *The Great Big Book of Jumbles* that contained thousands of anagrams of words of five and six letters. Each game consisted of four anagrams, some of whose letters were circled; after you solved the anagrams, you then had to solve the larger anagram of circled letters, the solution consisting of a pun hinted at in an accompanying cartoon.

"Time me," Jennie said as she began a jumble.

I timed her by the clock on the wall as she did three in a row. All four words and the pun solved in eleven seconds, nine seconds, twelve seconds.

It sometimes took me minutes to solve the four anagrams, and I was only rarely able, with help from her, to solve the pun. She was so much better at it than I was that she must have been bored each time I took my turn, but she pretended she was only better because she had had more practice.

She told me her favourite teacher had been a missionary nun from Peru named Sister Maura Clareta, who had given her a book of jumbles for her birthday one year.

"She was the sweetest woman," Jennie said. "All the boys and girls thought the world of her." When Sister Maura left St. Kevin's, Jennie agreed to name her first-born girl after her, so it was possible that the baby she was pregnant with now would be named Maura Clareta Johnston.

She told me about a riddle that Sister Maura had taught her. Later I found out it was actually Pascal's Wager, but she didn't know it was called that and, as far as I know, had never heard of Pascal—and the same, in both cases, seemed to have been true of Sister Maura.

"Some professor priest or something came up with this long ago," Jennie explained.

The riddle concerned a bet on whether or not you should believe in God. I was confused because I thought that everyone believed in God. I thought Dad was only pretending to think that the Bible wasn't true to get on Jennie's nerves.

She must have noticed that I was perplexed, because she assured me that Sister Maura hadn't taught her the riddle to convince her that God existed. It was just that she knew Jennie would admire its cleverness and have fun with it.

So Jennie told me the riddle. When I shrugged in bewilderment, she wrote it down: What harm would come to you from believing in God even if there was no God? You would lose nothing. But if there was a God and you *didn't* believe in Him, you would lose everything. If there was no God and you didn't believe in Him, what would you gain from being right? Nothing. If there was a God and you believed in Him, you would gain everything. So, your best wager, literally, was to believe in God. To bet on God.

I got it eventually, though I didn't really get the point of it. Still, I had the notion that, to Jennie, it was more than just a riddle.

She said that the riddle had gotten Sister Maura in trouble with the principal and the priest, who thought it wasn't right to make Faith the subject of a bet—it made Christians sound like gamblers. She wasn't sure what transpired between Sister Maura and the priest and the principal, but Sister Maura gained a reputation as an upstart who was too full of herself and had too many new ideas. In the end, she was sent back to Peru.

Jennie looked at what she had written, the riddle about God that a nun she was going to name her first girl after had taught her years ago. She smiled and said she really thought the riddle was smart and I said I did, too.

Next, she went to the kitchen, fished about in one of the upper cupboards and came back with what she said was her last report card. She handed it to me and I opened it. She'd got a hundred in mathematics. A hundred in English. Seventy-six in religion. But she'd failed all the other courses. She got between thirty-five and forty-five in geography, history, home economics, Latin, civics. My mother had failed grade ten.

She looked at me, waiting for my reaction. I didn't know what to say. She said she'd only gone to school that year because she was not old enough to go to secretarial school.

"Read what's written at the bottom," she said. I looked down to see a handwritten note from a Mr. Dempsey: "Jennie would do well to apply herself more as she does not possess much in the way of natural intelligence. She is a troublemaker and a terrible influence on others. I cannot help but speculate that her small stature may be an indication of some natural underdevelopment of the mind that would predispose her to failure in any attempt to further her education or to refine her character."

I told her I thought Mr. Dempsey sounded mean. She nodded and looked as if she was recalling the moment she had first read the words that still stung her after all this time. She welled up, so I put my arms around her neck and hugged her. She briefly patted my back as if to say that she was not as upset as she seemed to be.

When I sat down again, she said that Sister Maura had taught her English and math, which happened to be her favourite subjects, but Sister Maura had made them better. She talked about things she found interesting, whether others thought they were interesting or not. I told her she would have got high grades in everything if Sister Maura had been her only teacher.

"Maybe," she said. "I guess we'll never know."

She looked again at Pascal's Wager.

"I told that to your father once," she said. "He called it 'sophisticated trickery.' I said it was just for fun."

"It *is* fun," I said. "Tricks can be fun."

She frowned slightly but nodded.

"Sister Maura and I still write to each other," she said. "She knows the baby is on its way."

"That's good," I said.

Jennie said that Sister Maura's letters had come to a lot of addresses over the years. Almost thirty. But she had never asked why, and Jennie had never told her.

"I have an underdeveloped mind and I lack refinement of character," she said, looking at me as if the words were mine.

"No, you don't."

"I might be what's wrong with you," she said.

I didn't understand her. I was especially afraid to ask what she meant by *what's wrong with you*. I hated to think that she thought of me that way.

"What are we going to do with you, Wayne?" she asked, sighing.

"What do you mean?" I said, wondering who "we" were and what options they were considering, just as I had when Lucy had asked what they were going to do with me.

"It's just an expression. We can't throw you back like a fish, can we?"

"No," I said.

She laughed a little. "We can't get a refund."

"No."

She laughed louder. "We can't exchange you for one that works. We can't complain about false advertising. We can't say you were already gone off when we bought you like we do at the meat department."

She sounded like Lucy, now, but Lucy said things like that in a way that didn't make me wonder what she really meant.

"Maybe we could say they gave us batteries that wore out sooner than they should have."

I knew she was joking, but I knew that she would never joke that way with my brothers, especially Craig. Ken had once told me that Craig was her favourite. It felt like she was getting back at me for what Mr. Dempsey wrote about her. Or maybe because I'd seen what he had written.

"I must have knit you," she said. "Or someone must have. Lucy maybe. Lucy used to say that about me. 'I must have knit you, Jennie.' Maybe she still does, does she?"

I shook my head no, emphatically.

"She used to because I was so small. 'The runt of the litter.'"

"I'm the runt of the litter, too," I said.

"You are so far. You'd be the runt of any litter. Maybe. We'll see how number five turns out." Number five. She was placing her dashed hopes for me on number five.

"On top of that, you're high-strung like me. Higher strung."

"What's high-strung?"

"Jumpy. Nervous. Afraid of your own shadow. Though there's not enough of you to make a shadow."

"Yes, there is."

"We might make one between the two of us."

"I have a shadow."

"You *are* a shadow," she said.

I shook my head.

"We're a pair of oddballs, then, how's that?"

I shrugged.

"Lucy knit me and I knit you."

"Who knit Lucy?"

She let loose a laugh and a cough, cigarette smoke coming out of her nose and mouth. "The next time you see Lucy, ask her who knit her."

"I will," I said.

seven

The next Sunday morning, there was an early winter bliz-
zard raging, gusts of wind slamming against the side of
the house, rattling the windows and even the doors, and creating so many drafts I couldn't bear to crawl out from beneath
the blankets of the bedmobile. "We can forget church for
this week," Dad said, peering out a window. "I can't even see
the road."

We all knew he was hungover and making a doomed attempt
to head Jennie off.

Someone had to represent the family at Sunday Mass, Jennie
said, to which Dad replied that even Ned and Lucy wouldn't
venture out in this. Which Jennie said was all the more reason
that one of us should go. Dad said fine, they could send *me*
out, even though Tiny Tim would have a better chance of
making it to church alive. *Undersized, chronically sick little
boy perishes in a heroic effort to represent his family at Sunday*

Mass. Saint Wayne of the Goulds, the patron saint of What Will People Say?

I laughed along with my brothers but still reddened with embarrassment. I told myself I would give it a try if Jennie asked me to. I looked at my father, wondering what he and my brothers said about me when I wasn't there to hear them.

Dad asked what would happen if there was no one from the family at Sunday Mass. Father McGettigan would notice, Jennie said. Yes, Dad said, and so would a handful of people whose opinion she often swore she didn't care about. Jennie said that someone had to be there because the Everard family hadn't missed a Sunday Mass since the church was built a hundred years ago. Dad said this was the Johnston family, not the Everard family, and he wouldn't mind at all if we missed Mass, given that there was an eighty-mile-an-hour wind blowing and it was twenty below zero. Besides, the priest had probably cancelled Mass by now.

Jennie said Father McGettigan never cancelled Mass, and Dad said that was because he lived a hundred feet from the church, as did the nuns and some of the people that Jennie wasn't trying to impress. *They* could represent the human race at Mass, not the Johnstons.

"If you don't go, so help me God, I will," Jennie said, "and people will wonder what kind of man lets his wife go out in such a storm while he stays in bed." Jennie went to the porch and started putting on her winter clothes. Then Dad went to the porch and started putting on his.

"What man expects marriage to increase his chances of freezing to death?" he said, as he pulled on his snow boots and tied the hood of his coat so tight there was barely room for his cigarette to stick out through it. Every time he spoke, a puff of smoke came out of the hood.

He said he could have got a Master's degree. He should have a Master's of Science. But what was he doing instead? He was tied down, that's what he was doing, stuck in a dead-end job, a caricature of a scientist, a mere technologist in a white coat, not the Master of Science he should have been.

Jennie looked scared and so did my brothers. Brian's lower lip quivered. I didn't know—I'm not sure that even Jennie knew—what a Master's degree was. But I knew what the word Master meant. He could have been a Master, but he wasn't one because of us. How we had prevented this, I had no idea. Was it because of me that he was about to walk to church in a snowstorm and listen to the priest that he made fun of, instead of being a Master, instead of having a masterful life somewhere far away from us, from me especially?

He shouldered the door open and slipped out through the gap, the wind slamming the door shut behind him.

Jennie paced about the house for the next two hours, her arms folded when she wasn't holding a cigarette to her mouth, glancing at the door and the windows every time the wind gusted.

My brothers retreated to their room, and I sat on my bed in the living room and coughed, listening to the screeching whistle of the wind in the fireplace.

Finally, we heard Dad climb the front steps and we all ran out to greet him. His hood was a mask of ice. How he'd been able to see through it to find his way home, I had no idea.

"Thank God," Jennie said. "Were you the only person there?"

"Never made it," he said. He struck the ice mask with the heel of one gloved hand. Ice and snow fell to the floor. I'd never seen his face so red.

"You didn't go anywhere near the church," Jennie said. "I can smell the beer on your breath."

"I went as far as I could," he said. "Then I knocked on Eddie Hannaford's door and he let me in. He was having a beer so I had one, too. A couple. Then I came home. As God is my witness. Eddie said I was crazy just to be outside. He said I knocked a thousand years off my time in purgatory just by *trying* to make it to Mass. He said to tell you to go easy on me. His wife said to tell you that I put her husband to shame. I put every man in the Goulds to shame but only because of you. I was a credit to you, she said, because she knew that I wouldn't go to Mass when the sun was splitting the rocks if it wasn't for you. She said that men are all the same, including priests, who are only in it for the wine. If it wasn't for the wine, the priests would miss Mass, too. Why else do they have three Masses every Sunday morning? If not for the wine, they would sleep in through three Masses and leave a church full of women and children waiting for hours until they got fed up and went home.

"I'll go three times next week, Jennie. I'll go to eight and nine and eleven o'clock Mass no matter how many strange looks McGettigan gives me. I'll get a bunch of men together about this. We'll never have a beer again until we save enough to chip in on a snowplow. There'll be no excuses then . . ."

Jennie left him there in the porch, water spreading in a pool about his feet. When he had undressed to his inner clothes, he marched past us boys to the kitchen, where Jennie was sitting, smoking a cigarette.

"I'm swearing off church," Dad said. "I'm not going, never again, no matter what the weather is like."

"Fine," she said. "People will see us walking to church without you. They'll assume you're hungover."

"If I go to church, they'll know for certain that I'm hungover from the way I look, so it will be better if I stay home and keep them guessing—I might fool a few of them."

"Fine," she said. "Don't go. What a spectacle we'll be, the five of us. Ken will have to carry Wayne."

"Leave Wayne home with me from now on," Dad said. "More often than not, you have to lead him out of the church because he's coughing so much. Then you have to wait outside with him until Mass is over, where you smoke up a storm. That's a spectacle, too."

She said she wouldn't trust him to look after *her* if she got sick, let alone Wayne. If it was up to her, she wouldn't leave him alone with a cigarette for fear he'd burn the house down.

All the better to leave Wayne with him, he said. Given how often I'd watched them do it, I probably knew how to put out a cigarette. Or did she think I wasn't even good enough for that?

She said this wasn't about what Wayne was good enough for. It was about what *he* was good enough for, which had never been a very long list and now was shorter by one because he had given up church.

In the living room where we were listening, Craig put an arm around my shoulders. I knew they'd stop soon and Dad would go to church next Sunday and that, after Sunday dinner, they'd go to their room and close the door and turn the radio up loud.

Most of the snow was gone by the time I arrived at Lucy's the next morning. I parked the bedmobile across from the stove, then got down on my hands and knees by the daybed and lifted up the blanket to see Murchie.

"Hello, Murchie," I said when I saw his yellow eyes looking out at me from the darkness.

"If you're hoping he'll get used to you," she said, "you can forget it, because he's not used to me yet."

"He must get bored," I said.

"He's been gathering his strength for ten years," Lucy said. "God help us all when he decides what to do with it."

I had my three gulps of Quik. "Do you think Murchie would come out to watch me if I slurped it from a saucer?"

"He might come out," Lucy said, "but not to watch. You're not Ned."

As she poured jug after jug of water over me in the bathtub, I told her about Sunday morning. "She sent your father out in *that*?" she said. I nodded, hugging myself, teeth chattering.

"That's partly my fault," Lucy said. "I sent Ned out into some pretty bad storms for the same reason. It's what people used to do, but they aren't doing it as much anymore, so Jennie ought to let up a bit."

"She'll never let up," I said, and Lucy said I was right. Jennie would send Dad to Mass if the last church that was left was on the moon.

When Ned came in at lunchtime, he poured his tea onto his saucer and began to slurp it, and Murchie peeked out from beneath the daybed, the white blanket like a dollop of cream on his head. He crept halfway across the floor. Ned blew on his tea and Murchie's ears pricked up. Ned slurped some more and Murchie advanced a couple of inches, his yellow eyes growing wider. Lucy stamped her foot and Murchie retreated, disappearing under the daybed.

Ned yawned, at the same time saying, "Oh my, oh my, oh my."

Lucy and I wheeled my bed into the living room and let him have his nap.

That afternoon, while we were kneeling at the Shrine, Lucy told me that Ned used to drink a long time ago, before, during and after Leonard, but mostly after. He drank from wine bottles that had no labels on them and no wine inside them. Moonshine. No amount of it was enough to make him miss a day's work. He stashed the bottles all over the farm, indoors and outdoors, but he never took a drink in the house. He slept on the daybed every night for years. Their children kept their distance from him, but only just in case. The boys did what he told them to by way of work, which wasn't much because he didn't trust anyone to do anything as well as he could.

The boys became men, the girls became women, and all of them eventually left home. She missed having them around the house, but none of them lived very far away.

Then Ned disappeared for two weeks and came back sober. He hadn't had a drink since.

Lucy lit the votive candle. Shadows flickered on the faces of Mary and the Baby Jesus. Lucy crossed herself and said a prayer for Leonard, and I crossed myself and pretended to say one. Her lips moved slightly. She crossed herself again.

She said that Ned was a riddle, but before anyone could solve it, they had to figure out how to put Ned into words. It wasn't like he went around dropping hints or planting clues.

I told her about Pascal's Wager.

"There's no ifs, ands, buts or maybes when it comes to God," Lucy said. "He's right there in front of us in Mary's arms. He's in the Bible. That's all the proof I need. Jesus drove the money changers from the temple because they were cheaters, just like gamblers are, just like that man who made up that wager. There's nothing in the Bible about the Holy Family playing bingo at the parish hall once a week. People would think it was fixed if a miracle worker like Jesus won the jackpot."

eight

Now that winter was near, I rarely went outdoors, so keenly did I feel the cold. The few minutes it took me to walk to Lucy's or from Lucy's left me so enervated I barely had the energy to make it up the steps.

One Friday, a warm front moved in, this time not accompanied by a lightning storm. Dad had to visit fish plants on the Southern Shore the following Monday, so he drove home from work with Jennie in a Federal Fisheries car that he was allowed to use for the weekend as long as he paid a mileage fee.

My brothers cheered at the sight of the car, in which, they hoped, Dad would take them fishing the next day.

When Dad and Jennie came into the house, they cheered again when Dad said that, though it was late in the year for fishing, and technically illegal, the forest rangers were mainly concerned about hunters in the fall, so yes, he would take the boys to a prime lake that you could only reach by car from where we lived.

I would stay home with Jennie, who wouldn't venture far enough from the house to pick berries. She had been raised to believe that the woods were the domain of men and boys, and the house that of girls and women, but she was also afraid of the host of spectral entities that Lucy said the woods were full of.

Before sunrise the next day, my brothers got out of their bunkbeds as quietly as possible, trying not to wake me, though they did anyway because my bed was in the front room. I didn't let on that I was awake but watched them through half-open eyes as they gathered together their bamboo fishing poles and straw-woven baskets, their hip waders and tackle boxes. These things, like their baseball bats and gloves, their hockey sticks and skates, were the totems of a life I could not take part in.

I watched from the living room window as Dad bound my brothers' poles together and tied them, thick ends forward, to the handles on the passenger side of the car so that he and my brothers could only get in and out on the driver's side. As they drove off, the poles looked like jousting lances. Dad and Ken were in the front and Craig and Brian in the back, the rest of their gear stowed in the trunk, which was so full it wouldn't close all the way and had to be tied down with a piece of rope.

It was as if my brothers had grown up in another country whose customs and pastimes were nothing like those of my own.

They returned just before dark with an especially good catch of trout. Before he cleaned the fish, Dad arrayed them on newspaper on the kitchen table, grouping them according to whether they were his, Ken's, Craig's or Brian's—big, chubby lake trout, speckled trout, landlocked salmon parr. Many of the trout Craig caught were bigger than Dad's, something Dad proudly pointed out. Even Jennie admired the trout, though she couldn't bring herself to touch one, so Dad had to cook them as well. The others feasted on the trout while Jennie and I watched—neither of us could abide the taste of fish of any kind. Jennie winked at me now and then as if to say that she and I had better sense than to join them.

That night, as I lay on my bed in the living room, I heard Jennie and Dad raise their voices, though I couldn't make out the words. But when the rest of us came home from early Mass the next morning, Dad asked me if I would like to go fishing.

Even though I knew that Jennie was the one who had convinced him to take me, as she had a few times before, I eagerly accepted, even though Dad looked the very picture of put out.

Like Dad and my brothers, I had the most inexpensive of fishing gear—a bamboo pole with a single black hook at the end of fifteen feet of nylon line. But, even so, Dad was very serious about the maintenance, appearance and storage of it, along with all the other gear that fishing required.

Our bamboo poles, though cheap, were carefully chosen by Dad from a sports shop in St. John's, as were our fishing baskets, knapsacks and hip waders, though the latter two items were many times mended by Jennie. Dad was always on my brothers to keep their gear ship-shape, but he didn't require anything of me, as if it would have been pointless to teach me something I would never get the knack of or live long enough to appreciate. When, every so often, he took me fishing on my own, all he asked was that I not be too much of a nuisance. He couldn't stand the sight of me walking along with my fishing line unwound and my baited hook dragging behind me on the ground.

The lake that Dad and my brothers had fished on Saturday was too far from the road for me to manage, requiring a trek through thick woods and stretches of deep peat bogs that even Dad got stuck in sometimes. So Dad and I drove to the path that led to the gullies—a series of beaver ponds along a small feeder stream between two nearby lakes. The path that led to them was well-worn and not too steep.

We categorized the streams we had to ford on the way to the pond we wanted to fish as either twos or sixes. A two was a stream slow and shallow enough for me to wade across without Dad's help. Since we crossed it once on the way to the Gullies and once on the way back, it was a two. A category six meant he had to carry our baskets, knapsacks and bamboo poles across, then come back and carry me across in his arms—three crossings that would have to be repeated on the way back, so a total of six.

I ran ahead to see how swollen each stream was. I always hoped for a six because I liked it when he carried me—I liked the scrape of his cheek against mine and the smell of his cigarette smoke in the outdoors. I even liked the smell of whatever he was drinking. I knew that, when I ran ahead of him, he took the opportunity to remove a flask from somewhere and take a mouthful. Though I heard the sloshing of the liquor and the sigh that followed it, I never looked back.

I deemed every stream to be a six but was often overruled. When it turned out that the stream *was* a six, he said, "Jesus Christ, Brian could walk across that. You're like your mother, afraid of everything. You have no business being out here at all." I felt desolate when he said things like that, which he did more often the more he drank, seeming to think I could no longer hear him or that the words were in his head.

The weather turned cold and foggy, the fog the kind that wet you through as drizzle did. But Dad said never mind, because grey days were better than sunny ones, when you cast a moving shadow on the water that scared the trout away.

After crossing three streams that were sixes, meaning Dad had had to make nine crossings in total and would have to make nine more on the way back, we came to the first gully, which was too shallow to bother with. We followed the path on to the second, bigger one, much deeper, surrounded by boulders that were on the edge of the glacial moraine that ran like a river of rock beside the stream on which the beavers built their houses. We stored our gear behind one of the boulders, and then I chose a rock to fish from.

"Can you put the worm on by yourself?" Dad asked as he unwound the black nylon line from the thick end of his bamboo pole.

"*Yes*," I said, rolling my eyes. I had never been squeamish about baiting a hook, but he always asked. I also knew by heart the instructions he was about to give me. "If your line gets snagged on a branch, just sing out to me and I'll untie it for you," he said. "I'm going up to the third gully. You stay put."

"Okay" I said.

"If you pull in a trout and it comes off the line and ends up in the bushes behind you, just leave it. Don't go looking for it, because the bushes are wet. I'll find it for you. Don't bother a beaver if you see one. He won't bother you if you don't bother him."

"I *know*," I said.

I also knew he was going up to the third gully so that, unseen by me, he could drink from his flask, and so that, also unseen by me, he could catch in an hour a dozen or so of the little gully trout to augment the one or two I might catch so that, when we got home, we could pretend that I had caught them all. He had come up with this ruse long ago, supposedly to spare me the embarrassment of a meagre catch but really to minimize the amount of time he had to spend with me at the gullies and maximize the amount he could spend in the Crystal Palace on the way home while I waited for him in the car—to his mind the one upside to having to spend his Sunday with me. I was happy to go along with the ruse because I had never acquired the knack of knowing when to pull when a trout was biting. I usually did so too soon, jerking the worm and hook away just as the trout began to nibble.

Dad struck out for the third gully, shouting over his shoulder, "Stay put till I get back. We'll start a fire and boil up then." A cigarette in his mouth, his bamboo in one hand, his basket strap strung like a sash across his chest and shoulders, he leapt nimbly from rock to rock, skirting the edge of the water until he rejoined the stream and disappeared behind a stand of dark spruce trees.

For me, fishing consisted of keeping my eye on the bobber, the floating piece of cork that tipped or sank when a trout was nibbling at the worm. That was pretty much all I did, sit there and stare at the bobber. This was the only kind of fishing I could do, and not considered to be fishing by anyone over the age of five.

Even though the gullies teemed with small trout, most of them too small to keep, I managed to catch very few of them. Over the next hour or so, I caught one that was so small it came off the hook when I pulled it in and went flying into the woods behind me. I imagined Dad upstream from me, sitting on a rock at the edge of the third gully, smoking and sipping from the flask of whisky, catching a trout when he felt like it, but mostly just revelling in the solitude.

The gullies, though small, were very deep, the water so black that, even when it was perfectly calm, you couldn't see the bottom. Although the gully trout were beautiful, dark black on the top with bright-red bellies, no one ate them, because they tasted of these brackish pools in which, except at spawning season, they were more or less trapped. Toy trout, Craig called them.

They *were* toy trout, and I soon lost interest in what the bobber was doing. Soaked through by the drizzle and looking forward to the fire that Dad would soon build, I felt the coming on of the curious drowsiness that always attended my getting too cold. It felt pleasant even though I began to shiver.

I put aside my bamboo and lay back on the rock, looking up at the cloud-like, rolling fog. A crow flew over. The fog parted briefly, and I caught a glimpse of the sun. Then the fog closed in again. I was soon in the twilight between sleep and wakefulness—the closest thing to real sleep I ever got, even while lying in bed.

I opened my eyes when it began to rain, lightly at first, scattered drops pattering on my forehead, my cheeks and on my lips, the water tasting faintly of salt. I heard the plopping of larger raindrops in the water. From upstream, Dad shouted something I could not make out. The rain suddenly became a downpour that drummed in the gully. I sat up, intending to stand, but instead, ever so slowly, I began to slide down the rock. I pressed the heels of my waders and the palms of my hands against the rock, but on I slid toward the water, which looked like it was boiling, so heavy had the rain become.

My feet went under, then my knees and thighs until the water reached my jeans and I felt the jolting cold of it as it poured into my waders and bubbled up around my crotch. I slid faster and shot off the rock, all of me hitting the dark murk of the gully, going under water in which I could see nothing, only feel myself sinking. And then, as if my jacket collar had snagged on the underwater trunk of a dead tree, my descent to the bottom stopped, my jacket and shirt came up around my face—and I slowly began to rise until I heard myself gasping as my head surfaced.

My slow ascent continued, my body sliding back up the rock, each successive part of me scraping its rough surface until nothing but my lower half was still submerged—at which point, my heavy, water-filled waders were sucked off me and sank out of sight.

For what seemed like a long while, I heard someone whelping like a seal. It was me, hyperventilating from the shock of the cold water, from terror and surprise.

I had no idea how I'd emerged from the water until I felt myself rising into mid-air and then being slung, face down, over what I realized was Dad's shoulder. I tried to say, "I lost my waders," but I couldn't get out a word. It occurred to me I must have lost my hat. My breathing gradually slowed, and I began to shiver, my heart racing round in my chest as if in a panic to find a way out, to get out of me to somewhere else, anywhere else.

"You're all right, you're all right," Dad kept saying, as if he was trying to convince himself that it was true. He ran with me over his shoulder, even as the rain pelted down so hard the gully sounded like river rapids. He took me to the other side, where there were bigger trees and an outcrop of rock that we had sheltered under once before when it snowed. Putting me down on my sodden socks, he crouched in front of me and placed his hands on my shoulders. He looked as wet as I felt, his hair matted to his head, water dribbling down his face.

"What in the name of Christ were you doing lying on a rock in the rain?"

I had no words for the warm weariness that had come over me on the rock even as I was shivering in the drizzle. He shook me for an answer and I began to bawl.

He took me in a tight hug, then held me away from him again and looked into my eyes in a way he had never done before, with terror, confusion, disbelief and guilt.

"Sit down under that," he said, pointing to a nearby outcrop of rock. "It's two hours back to the car. More if this rain keeps up and those streams overflow. We've got to get you warm and dry your clothes. I'll make a fire. It's a bit damp, but I could get a fire going underwater if I had to."

I imagined that, imagined looking down at the gully from the rock that I'd been perched on, watching the faint flicker of a flame starting up in all that darkness, like the momentary flash of the scarlet belly of a gully trout. Lucifer the Light Bringer, who had found fire in the Deep and brought it up into the world, a near-limitless journey that he had made entirely alone. His name was like Lucy's.

I felt a wave of dizziness and pitched forward, luckily landing on my side. I managed to right myself before Dad, who was casting about for dry wood, noticed what had happened.

There was a circle of scorched, soot-covered stones on the ground that many others must have used. "When the fire gets going, take off everything but your underwear," he said, carrying back his armful of wood. "You can wear my jacket. It's reversible."

"Someone might see me," I said.

"No one will see you. Anyone else who was out in this has sense enough to be headed home by now. You'll have my jacket on. You'll be all right with it zipped up."

"My waders are in the gully," I said. "I don't know where my cap is."

"You can wear my cap. The waders will have to stay where they are. You've nothing for your feet so I'll have to carry you out. Jesus, what a fuck-up."

89

I'd never heard him use the word before.

"I'm sorry," I said.

"You'll be sorrier if you catch pneumonia," he said. "At least you're not coughing. That's a good sign, right?"

I nodded.

"I swear to God, who hasn't got sense enough to duck into the woods when it rains? What were you thinking?"

Shivering in my wet clothes, I watched him build the fire, starting with some kindling and newspaper he had brought in his basket.

"Stay clear of the smoke," he said. I knew he was worried that I'd start coughing. I was surprised that I hadn't. He found some dead orange spruce boughs. I took off my clothes and he gave me his jacket, then spread my clothes out on some flat rocks near the fire.

"They'll dry in no time," he said, as if he was still trying to reassure himself that it was true, that things were under control again and he might not be blamed.

We were soon seated round a roaring blaze. I felt the heat of it on my face and on my bare legs and feet. I felt better, so much so that I fancied that something could still be salvaged from the day.

"Let's boil up," I said, and his face softened.

He took the flask of whisky from his pocket. It was still half-full. He took a swallow. He didn't care, now, that I could see him drinking. By the time we got back to the Goulds, it would be too late for him to stop at the Crystal. He, too, was trying to salvage something from the day. He put the cap back on the flask.

"All right, we'll boil up," he said. "Why not? We'll get some hot tea into you. That was a close one you had, wasn't it?"

"It was really close," I said. "The closest one yet."

I could tell that he didn't like me saying that, me who had come close so often that coming close was what I was best known for in the Goulds. He thought that I was rubbing it in.

"You didn't hear me calling out, for Christ's sake?"

I pretended I hadn't, shaking my head and trying to look surprised.

"I had my eyes on you the whole time," he said. "I never let you out of my sight. I kept waiting for you to sit up. If I hadn't headed your way when it started to rain—" He made a great show of shaking his head at the thought of what would have happened. He took the flask out again and took two swallows, grimacing as his Adam's apple went up and down. I knew there'd be no boiling up if he drank much more, and I wondered if he had another flask in his basket.

"Let's boil up, okay?" I said.

Boiling up was what I had always liked most about going to the gullies, eating the lunch he heated for me over a fire that he built.

He made tea in a large apple juice can from which the top had been removed and which bore a handle fashioned from a coat hanger. Along with the tea, he heated brown beans in the can and toasted the bologna sandwiches that Jennie had packed for us.

The plunge into the gully, the cold, and now the heat of the fire, the outdoor air and the smell of woodsmoke gave me a false appetite and I ate with gusto.

I gorged myself, making Dad, who was sitting on a rock beside me, smile at me in spite of himself because he knew what was coming as well as I did.

What always happened, happened this time with a vengeance. I managed to get up and turn my back to him before I brought it all back up, every bit of what had tasted so good going down. Why was I even capable of being ravenous if this was always the result? Why was I forever giving in to this trick my body played on me? It was like when he was drinking. He was always unhappy, even sad, bored with everyone and everything, yet seemingly convinced that, if he drank more, these feelings would go away.

He asked me, his tone accusatory, why Jennie made and packed so much food for me. I said she made it for the two of us, and most of it for him, even though she knew he wouldn't take a bite because he didn't eat when he was drinking. I said I should have stopped when I ate as much as I could stomach, but I couldn't help myself because it tasted so good. It wasn't his fault or hers. It was mine because my stomach was the size it had been when I was born, the size of a child's fist. Lucy had once said that to me.

"I don't know why Jennie sends you off with so much food," he said as if he hadn't heard my explanation. "She knows you can't keep it down."

"Sometimes I can," I protested. "I really *like* it. I don't know why it comes back up. Maybe today I do, though. Maybe it's because I fell in." I wasn't going to let him off easy. Today, my words implied, in light of what had happened—what would not have happened but for him—it was entirely to be expected that I would eat too much food too fast and bring it all back up. But he was only getting started.

"I can't help it if you have no better sense. I take your brothers fishing, and then I have to take you by yourself. It's like we have a girl in the family. The boys do one thing, the girl does something else, and I'm the one who has to mind the girl."

"I'm not a girl."

"I caught a fine basketful of trout for you. I always do, and who gets the credit?"

"Jennie knows the trout aren't mine, and the boys do, too."

"They're *your* trout," he said.

"They're toy trout," I said. "Nobody eats them. Jennie leaves them in the fridge for a while and then she throws them out. Everyone pretends. I do, too."

He sighed and his shoulders slumped. He looked into the fire and, as if he was talking to it, he said no, it was his fault and he would make it up to me someday, he swore he would, because he liked me as much as he liked the other boys even if it sometimes seemed he liked me less. "Never mind about it," he said, with so much tenderness in his voice that I began to bawl again.

He took me in his arms. "There's nothing wrong with pretending now and then. It's not your fault that you're not cut out to catch trout. It's not like it's a mortal sin. It's just the way you are. You can't help it. It's not your fault and it's not my fault."

He let go of me and we both stared into the fire, which was starting to die down.

"We won't tell Jennie that you went all the way under, all right? Or that you were by yourself on the rock, or why? We'll just say that you fell in up to your waist. Just up to your waist near the shore. We'll have to say that much because of your cap and your waders. Why we came back without them, right? We'll say your waders got stuck in the mud and came off when you climbed out, and we couldn't find them because they drifted out to where that water was too dark, all right?"

"All right."

"She doesn't know anything about the woods or anything like that. She won't know the difference. It will be our secret."

"Ken and Craig, *they* know the outdoors. They'll ask me about it, especially Craig. He'll worm it out of me."

"Only if you let him."

"He will."

"If he does, he won't tell Jennie. He's not a tattletale."

"I'm not, either."

On the way out, we discovered that the sixes had become too deep to cross so we had to walk a long way upstream to where there was a kind of bridge fashioned from old telephone poles lashed together with rope. He carried me across in his arms, jumping from side to side instead of trying to balance on one pole. The poles were wet and his feet slipped between them from time to time.

"Sixes," he said. "Jesus Christ. This is more like a twenty."

It was well past dark by the time we got home.

❧

"We were held up by the weather," Dad told Jennie, and my brothers, all of whom came out of the bunk room when they heard us clumping up the back steps.

Jennie had me sit beside her on the chesterfield, where she pored over me again and again, feeling my hair, patting my clothes, squeezing different parts as if to see if they were injured or still there. Dad told the story that we had agreed on—I had fallen partway into the gully and then scrambled out, losing my waders.

When Dad was done, Jennie said, "You took Wayne fishing and you brought him home with nothing on his feet but socks?"

"The waders were all we had with us," Dad said. "How was I supposed to know he would lose them in the gully?"

Jennie said I smelled as if I had fought my way home through a forest fire.

"We dried his clothes by a fire after he fell in," Dad said.

"You stripped him down in the middle of the woods?"

"What choice did I have? I couldn't let Wayne catch his death in wet clothes, especially given how cold a day it was."

"He's wet *now*," Jennie said.

"Because of the *rain*," Dad said, a note of defeat creeping into his voice.

"So you dried his clothes by the fire and then put his clothes back on and took him out into the pouring rain where he got soaked to the skin again. Soaked to the skin is as wet as you can get. What was the point of the fire?"

"He warmed up for a while beside the fire," Dad said. "He warmed up on the inside. That was better for him than us heading straight home after he fell in. He should be having a warm bath now, not sitting there on the chesterfield in wet clothes."

It had been hours since he had had a drink. He was probably hungover. The way he looked made me wonder how I looked.

Craig asked me how many trout I caught. I didn't know how many Dad had caught for me, so I said I didn't know how many were in the basket because some might have washed away when I fell in the gully.

"Washed away?" Craig said, laughing. "There's no current at all in those gullies. They're just dead pools. How could your trout wash away?"

I had blundered, so embarrassed was I to admit to what the others *already* knew, that Dad caught most of my trout for me. I looked to Dad to help me save face. He looked trapped.

"You three," Jennie said to my brothers, "go to your room and close the door." As they were leaving, Craig flashed me a murderous look.

Jennie must have seen that I was ripe for the taking. She put her hands on my shoulders and turned me to face her.

"What happened?" she asked. "How did you fall in? No more lies."

All I had to do was own up to what everyone in the family already knew, that it was Dad who caught most of my trout. But I wanted to get even with Dad, so I started bawling and began to tell her what had happened at the gully.

Dad interrupted me. He told her the truth—not all of it but most of it. He said that he'd been drinking—likely because Jennie would have supplied that detail anyway—but didn't say that he'd gone up to the third gully to be by himself. I was surprised that he left that out, as he must have worried that I would tell her.

Jennie greeted his confession with silence. She told me to take a bath, change into a dry set of clothes, wheel my bed into the bunk room and stay there.

We heard them talking in the kitchen from behind the closed door of the bunk room. I knew it would be my turn after Jennie was through with Dad. She wouldn't rip into me, but Craig would.

So Dad had almost let me drown while he was getting drunk, she said. How did I fall in that far, that deep? Wasn't he keeping an eye on me at all?

Dad said I slid right off the rock like I was on a shoot-the-chute. It happened that fast. There was nothing he could do but what he did, which was save my life by grabbing me and pulling me out before I went in so deep they would have had to drag the dark gully just to find my little body.

My little body. I looked at Craig when Dad said that, but Craig's eyes were closed. I had seen men dragging the pond down the road from our house once, looking for the body of a man who had fallen from a boat.

She said where was Dad when I went in?

Dad said he was right beside me, so help him God, because he never went far away from me, because I couldn't look after myself in the woods like the other boys could.

She asked him what he had to drink, and he said some Royal Reserve.

How much?

Only what was left in a flask he had taken with him from the house, he insisted.

Why did he have to get drunk to go fishing with his son? Was it that much of a burden? Or was he always drinking when she was not around? Did he go into the woods just to get away from her so he could drink?

No.

Did he drink when he went fishing with the other boys?

A little bit sometimes, he said, but fishing with the other boys was different. Brian was already better at it than Wayne would ever be.

My eyes stung with tears. I felt like going out and telling Jennie about him leaving me alone downstream, and the stupid fire that I sat beside, wearing nothing but his jacket and his hat while he went on drinking, and the sandwiches and beans and the tea that came back up, and how cold the water was when I fell in and went all the way under where it was so dark I couldn't see, and the way my heart hopped around inside my chest while I tried to catch my breath.

Jennie told him to keep his voice down, and for a while we couldn't hear them but then their voices rose again.

Could he put his hand on his heart and tell her that this would have happened whether he was sober or not?

Yes, he could because, if he was sure of nothing else, he was sure that it had been an accident that not even a stone cold sober man could have foreseen, let alone prevented.

He was worthless, he knew it, and it should have been him who had fallen in, not Wayne, who, at the best of times, had it worse than any child he'd ever known, what with his being such a runt and coughing all the time and dragging his bed around the house like some kind of pet. He wondered if he might be remembered, if he would be remembered at all, which he knew he had less right to expect than the least mosquito—but still he wondered if he might be accorded some scintilla of credit for *something*, he didn't know what, he honestly didn't, but was there nothing about him such as that he had saved his son's life that might inspire someone to put a lone check mark on the credit side of the ledger that contained the record of his soul?

The tide had changed, as it always did. Now Jennie would start to pick up for him, and Ken and Craig and Brian might go out to the kitchen and join her in trying to convince him that he ought not to forget that he was a better man than most, just as he ought not take his flaws so much to heart that he sought escape in drink, seeing as how there were so many men more flawed than him who were so devoid of a conscience that they *never* took a drink . . . But I would not go out there. I would stay in the bunk room the way he stayed in the bedroom when we said the rosary.

Jennie did start in on his defence, but my brothers stayed put. Craig, who had been standing facing his bunk, turned away from it and looked down at me, leaning propped on my elbow in the bedmobile.

"Fell in *and* lost your cap *and* lost your waders," Craig said. I nodded. "You could have kept your mouth shut," he said. "You didn't have to start bawling and telling on Dad. Now he's telling on himself. Sook."

He kept ripping into me, as if the way I was caused Dad to be the way he was, and everyone to be the way they were, and every*thing* to be the way it was.

He and Ken held my hand only because Jennie told them to, he said. She didn't tell them to hold Brian's, but she told them to hold mine. He bet that Brian could beat me up.

He said I turned up my nose at everything Jennie cooked. That was why I was so sickly, except that half the time I only pretended to be sick so I wouldn't have to *do* anything.

He said Dad spent the rent because I was such a nuisance. My stupid bed had wheels on it. Nobody's bed had wheels. Because of me, we had to live in this lousy house and we'd soon be living somewhere worse.

Mom's nerves were shot because she worried so much about me.

He punched his pillow over and over, as if he would have done the same to me if I wasn't such a dork. His face was contorted with bitter rage, his eyes full of tears. He said that Jennie might not let Dad take him and Ken and Brian fishing again because of me. He shook his fist in my face. Then I would *really* be in trouble.

If anything else went wrong because of me, he warned, I'd be sent to a home for people who couldn't take care of themselves, and I'd never get out. They had such homes in St. John's. How could Jennie look after the baby that was on the way and look after me? Who'd look after me when I was forty? That's what these homes were for, and that's where I'd go if I got worse.

That's when I started bawling.

His tone changed. "You're not going to end up in a home." He said it as if he was amused and charmed by how given I was to fearing that such things would happen to me. I wasn't going to be sent to a home, or die in my sleep, or wind up in a wheelchair.

He hugged me, too, laughing as though at my endearing fretfulness, and I clung to him as if, without him, without my older brother, I'd be lost. I loved him for defusing the bomb that he had planted in my mind.

When I started bawling even harder, he said, "Oh, for *frig's* sake!"

Ken told him to leave me be. Craig lay down on my bed and gave me another hug. "I was just kidding with you," he said. "Don't you know when someone's kidding with you?"

I nodded and went on bawling, which got him laughing and hugging me even harder.

I spent the night in the living room. My cough started up, but still I fell into a kind of sleep, and then into a fitful dream. My chattering teeth made the sound of a sewing machine. Down, down into the water I slid until my head was under and everything was dark and cold. Then up, up. My clothes sagged and clung to me, becoming heavier as I rose out of the water that I couldn't see and slithered backward up the rock. Then down, down again.

Jennie wanted me to tell her what had happened and, until I did, the rising and the falling would continue. Into the water, out of the water. Tell me, tell me, or I will hold you under till you drown—a threat never made good on, for I kept coming back, rising slowly to the surface like a trout that had been hooked.

nine

The next day, while pouring jugs of water on my head in the bathtub, Lucy said that my shoulder blades were so sharp it was a wonder they didn't pop through the skin. My Adam's apple rose and fell, rose and fell, like a bingo ball. My legs were twigs. I was so small I should be wearing hand-me-ups from Brian. She could see my heart pulsing like a frog's throat in my chest. She didn't like the look of me. What kind of bath had I had the day before that I was still smelling as Ned did when he came back from a week in the woods? The Sunlight soap that stung my eyes was the one thing that could take away that smell. "Keep still," she said as she scoured my body, the block of soap so big she could barely hold it in her hand. "I'll never get this smell of bog out of your hair. I'll have to send you home bald."

That's when I told Lucy everything that had happened the day before.

"So he sat you on a rock and left you there. Where did your father go after he sat you on that rock?"

"He went up to the next gully."

"That's like telling me he went to Mars. I've never seen a gully in my life. If you can't think of anything better to do with one than slide into it and drown, I guess I haven't missed much.

"He loves his privacy, your father does. Up to the next gully, whatever that is, and what odds about you. If he ever loses a youngster, God forbid, he might pay more attention to the ones he still has left.

"Men going into the woods in droves. What for? It's a long way to go to have a drink and a smoke. Men traipsing around in the woods, mistaking each other for moose. A man down the road chased his own youngster out of the woods last fall. Shot at him five times before he caught on. The youngster hasn't left the house since."

When she was done scrubbing me, she vigorously dried me with a towel. "I'm trying to rub some colour into you," she said. "You look like evaporated milk."

I pictured the yellowish milk coming out of a can and felt a wave of dizziness, but I managed to keep my balance.

"Let's go in to see Mary and the Baby Jesus," Lucy said. I followed her to the bedroom, which seemed even darker than usual.

"You light the candle," she said, offering me the box of matches. My hands shook too much to slide the box open.

"When did that start?" Lucy said. "You weren't like that when you got here, were you? You weren't like that in the tub or when I dried you off, were you?"

I shook my head.

"I've seen drunks that didn't have the shakes that bad."

I tried again to open the box but couldn't.

"Here," she said, "I'll do it, or else you'll still be at it when Ned comes home for lunch."

"I know how to light a match."

"Then this must be the one match you *don't* know how to light."

She took the box back, slid it open and removed a match. She lit it and then the candle. The flame flickered as if there was a draft. I looked up at Lucy and she blessed herself.

"Your head is going up and down a mile a minute," she said. "And look at your arms. They're all goosebumps."

"I don't want any Quik today," I said.

"So you said when you got here. And twice since then. Do you feel sick?"

"A bit."

"You always feel a *bit* sick. Is it worse than that?"

"It's different."

"Different? You've had everything there is to have three times over, unless I'm overlooking something you've only had twice. Is there some part of you that hurts?"

"No," I said.

She pressed the back of her hand to my forehead. "You don't have a temperature," she said. "Not on the *warm* side of normal, anyway."

"I'm all right," I said.

"Think about something other than being sick. I'll tell you about this statue. My mother got it from *her* mother as a wedding present. Mom set it up in the front room. That wasn't all that unusual back then. There was a time when almost everyone had a statue of some kind in their house. If it wasn't Mary and the Baby Jesus, it was the Sacred Heart or Jesus on the Cross. I wonder where all those statues went. It wouldn't be easy to get rid of one on the sly, but you wouldn't want to be seen heading to the dump with one. I suppose you could put it in a brin bag and weight it down with rocks and toss it in a pond. There must be a lot of them hidden away somewhere. I bet that more than one person has got a good fright when they found Jesus on the Cross behind the furnace of a house they just moved into. Nowadays people think you're off your rocker if you have one *anywhere* in the house, but it's only odd if you think of it as a knick-knack. I sometimes wonder who'll keep this Shrine going when I'm gone. Not Ned. He'd probably make a scarecrow out of it. God knows where it will end up if I leave it to one of my children. Buried under something in their basement. At the rate that you crowd move from house to house, I can't see Jennie convincing Art that they should lug it all over the Goulds like a member of the family in the back of Ned's truck every time you move to another house, can you?"

"No."

"Do you still feel different?"

"Yeah."

"You *look* different. Worse than you did when you got here. Well, we'll kneel down and say a prayer to Mary and the Baby Jesus. If they'll still listen to me after all the jokes I told about them just to cheer you up. Now help me kneel down."

She always leaned on me for balance when she was getting to her knees, but this time when she put her hand on my shoulder, I gave way.

"Jesus, Mary and Joseph," she groaned when one of her knees and then the other hit the floor.

"Sorry," I said.

"That's all right," she said. "As long as you don't pass out altogether and I'm stuck here on my knees until Ned gets home. It's better that you went sideways than headfirst—for the sake of your head, I mean, not the statue. There might be something in creation you pose a threat to, but that statue isn't it.

"Here," she said, taking my hand. "I'll lower *you* down."

I began to kneel, inching down bit by bit.

"Will you be all right if I let go?" she said.

"I think so," I said. When she released me, I tipped forward slightly, mesmerized by the flame inside the frosted glass. I righted myself just as she grabbed my shoulder.

"There you are," she said. "We'll look at the pictures, say a short prayer and then get you home to Jennie." Jennie, too, had been worried by the look of me that morning and had stayed home just in case I took a turn.

I looked at Leonard, then at Ned. How happy they seemed to be making each other in that moment, how unconcerned, how lighthearted, though Leonard was already sick and Ned must at least have suspected.

For the first time, Lucy flipped the photo over. "Leonard and Ned, August, 1936," someone had printed in pencil. "Leonard," Lucy said, "died on December 14, twelve days after his eighth birthday."

Lucy tapped the photo.

"His last birthday was a sad day in the house. We knew, everyone in the Goulds knew, that his time was short. He was waked in the house from the 15th to the 18th, when he was buried. He died eleven days before Christmas. Christmas Eve, Christmas Day, Boxing Day, New Year's Eve, New Year's Day. A sad month. There was hardly a sound in the house. He's why I keep up the Shrine. You're too young to know what it was like back then. What it was like for Ned and me and the youngsters. None of us forget, though some of us act like we do."

Lucy hated the thought that the Shrine to Leonard would end with her, and perhaps hated, too, that no one would kneel in front of it to look at a photograph of her, to remember Lucy fondly and wistfully and without grief because so much time had passed since she had died. But I felt *relief* that no photo of me would ever be a part of Lucy's Shrine, ever be among those laid out at the feet of Mary and the Baby Jesus and prayed over by someone who looked forward to dying and going to heaven as much as Lucy seemed to do. She turned the photo over again.

All this time I'd thought Leonard was smiling, but I realized he wasn't, really. He was overdressed for the weather in some sort of homemade outfit, none of his hair showing, just his face framed by what now looked to me like a bathing cap. His forehead seemed to be marred by a birthmark. There might even have been blood on his lips, unless these were blemishes owing to the age of the photograph. I couldn't understand why I'd never noticed them before.

Lucy bowed her head and blessed herself. I did the same just as my legs gave way, causing me to sit back on my heels, then topple onto my backside.

"God Almighty," Lucy said.

"I think I'll go home now," I said.

I managed, with Lucy's help, to get out of the house and across the road. Jennie, who had seen through the front window the apparition of Lucy, outdoors and barefoot, holding one of my arms with both her hands as I staggered homeward like a drunk, met us at the front door.

It was after supper, and Dad and the boys were watching TV. Craig had retrieved the bedmobile from Lucy's and I had been semi-reclined on it ever since, coughing more and more until the cough became so constant I may as well have been a dictator orating to a massive audience, exhorting them to sacrifice themselves to some lunatic cause.

Ordinarily, I'd have been banished to the bunk room by now, my coughing muffled enough for them to hear the TV, but sounds of a sort that alarmed even Dad had been coming from my chest. Jennie had rubbed me with Vicks VapoRub to no effect except to bring stinging tears to my eyes.

Now she was sitting on the floor by my bed, watching me as intensely as the others were watching TV. She cringed every time my bark reached a higher pitch. She held my hand, squeezing it now and then, her other hand adjusting the cold compress she'd put on my forehead.

"God Al*mighty*, did you hear that?" she said to my dad.

The only thermometer in the house was broken, so Jennie tried to gauge my temperature by placing her hand on my forehead, but I swatted it away as if her ministrations were the cause of all my pain. I heard what I was certain was the rasping of a wood saw. I tried to expel crushed gravel from my lungs.

Then Jennie said that I was soaking wet—"Look at the sweat just pouring off him!"—and I thought she wanted me to strip down to my shorts so that she could dry my clothes beside a fire she had built. Soon, other hands joined hers to make sure that I didn't. I was freezing and couldn't understand why the way to fix this wasn't obvious to everyone. I heard myself say that I could build a fire underwater if I had to. Then I heard Craig laugh and say something that made the others laugh. Leonard stared at me, his mouth stained with blood. Only months later, most of which he spent on his back in bed, he died. My brothers would remember Jennie pulling the sheet up to cover my face.

Someone got a fire going. We were boiling up despite the rain. We used the tea-coloured water from the gully to make tea that tasted smoky. I ate the steaming beans with a spoon, straight from the can, and the beans were smoky, too. The paper on the tin turned black like the beans at the bottom of the can. And then I ate the sandwiches. The tea and beans were hot, but the sandwiches were cold. The best way to eat bologna was when everything was cold, the mustard and the butter and the bread, but especially the slices of bologna that Jennie cut the night before, peeling off the wax. She made the sandwiches and put them in the fridge but they were even colder when I ate them in the woods, so cold they hurt my teeth until I took a swig of tea and everything got mixed up in my mouth, hot and cold, and smoky milk in smoky tea, and all of it went down my throat into my belly—

I came out of the dream needing to throw up. I managed to scramble off the cot and, with Craig's help, made it to the toilet, which I bent over just as a great gush came pouring out of me.

"Kneel down," Craig said. I did. The first gush was followed by another. Craig moved his hand in soothing circles on my back just as he always did. His hand seemed to say that I needn't feel ashamed, that he never did when he was sick, and he'd been sick more often than I ever had, and every time felt worse than I was feeling now.

"That's it, get it out of you," I heard him say in his voice of experience. "You'll feel better soon."

I was sick again and again. Nothing that came up looked like anything I had ever had to eat or drink in my entire life.

"God, Jennie," Craig shouted. "I think he's getting worse."

It was as if my insides had liquefied. I was hollow but for what was pouring out of me. Everything was lime green, the colour of popsicles I'd seen but never tasted. What I took to be a swarm of little black mosquitoes momentarily appeared, then went away. A popsicle-stick tongue depressor went in too far, pushed down too hard on my tongue. Another gush of sick. Then the throwing up stopped.

The mosquitoes came back and I tumbled onto my side. I felt the cool linoleum of the bathroom floor against my cheek. My body seemed to rise up on its own, or else my soul was leaving me. I felt a pair of hands under my armpits and another pair beneath my knees.

I found the strength to squirm and wriggle out of the grip of those sinister hands and fell, knocking my upper front teeth hard on the bathroom sink on my way down to the floor.

"He broke his friggin' teeth," Craig shouted.

Where was Jennie?

Ken and Craig each took hold of one of my forearms and tried to either pull me to my feet or drag me from the bathroom.

"He's too weak."

Dad's voice.

Wayne had always been too weak. Something like this was bound to happen sooner or later. A fire underwater. Up, up from the Deep, surfacing from the bottom of a gully as dark as the sea, Lucifer came, a speck of light so small that only God, peering down into the Deep, could see it. The Light Bringer holding his torch aloft, the great archangel summoned by the God whose Love he was destined to betray.

He took me in his arms and carried me from the bathroom to the living room and laid me on my bed.

I tongued the edges of my broken teeth and tasted blood. The blood on Leonard's lips, the expression on his face that I had taken for a smile. Ned was sharpening his scythe. The Grim Reaper in the sunny meadow with his little boy.

I woke again. "I got it out of me," I said.

"I'm calling Dot Chafe," I heard Jennie say. Dot Chafe, the nurse who lived nearby. I liked Dot.

She arrived with a first aid kit and put a thermometer in

my mouth, then took it out. "Oh, Sacred Heart of Jesus," she said. "This boy is very sick."

"Do we need an ambulance?" Dad said.

"You can call one, but it won't get here in time," Dot said. "They take at least an hour no matter what you tell them."

"Well, what *should* I tell them?" Dad said.

Jennie said I wasn't going to the hospital, because no one who had ever gone to the hospital from the Goulds came back alive.

"Call one, Art," Dot said. Jennie whispered something, and soon all three of them were whispering. Still, I heard Dad ask Jennie if she would sooner have me die than admit I was sick enough to need an ambulance. Then Dot said, "Go ahead, Art," and Jennie started crying.

I didn't mind them talking about me like that. I don't think I would have minded if Dot had said there was no hope. I was too weak to care about death's door. I'd always been too weak to care. Too slow. Fast enough to catch my death but nothing else. Lucy had said that about someone, not about me.

"We need ice," Dot said. "We have to bring his temperature down. Take off his clothes and put him in the tub and fill it with cold water and ice, as much ice as you can find."

Dad carried me back to the bathroom and sat me on the toilet cover, propping me up, his hands on my shoulders, while Jennie, still crying, hands shaking, removed my pajamas.

"His underwear, too," Dot said.

Jennie slid them off. Dad laid me in the empty tub and turned the cold water on full force.

"I've only got six ice cubes in the house," Jennie said.

"Go up and down the road, the five of you, and tell them you need every cube of ice they have," Dot said. "Go. I'll look after him."

I saw my brothers in the doorway. Brian was crying, and Ken and Craig looked at me with what I imagined was the kind of awe you feel the first time you see someone soon to die.

"Get GOING," Dot said. "I could fry an egg on his forehead. We have to bring his temperature down or he'll have brain damage or worse."

"Don't go to Lucy's, though," Jennie said. "You'll scare the life out of her."

My family scattered. Drops of sweat fell from my forehead onto my chest and I began to shiver. I tried to climb out of the tub, but Dot held me down.

What happened for the next little while on Petty Harbour Road has often been recounted, sometimes by me, though all I have ever done is repeat what I was told.

My family hurried from house to house, making their case for ice on the doorsteps of people they had gotten out of bed, who then got their families out of bed to help mine.

Brian told people that I was in the bathtub, but it wasn't cold enough to stop what was damaging my brain. But he couldn't leave off crying, so Jennie sent him home.

People gave every cube of ice they had, then ran every which way on Petty Harbour Road, often trying houses that others had already tried or that were empty because their owners were elsewhere scavenging for ice.

Telephone calls criss-crossed the length of Petty Harbour Road: Jennie's boy was in danger. Dot Chafe had said that, unless his temperature came down, he would die or never be the same again. At the same time as they earnestly took part in the search for ice, more than one person joked that, given how I had fared so far, my never being the same again might be for the best.

Grown-ups and children bearing boilers, bowls, buckets, ice trays, saucepans and all manner of other containers converged on the house in which the boy for whom some such end as they were trying to stave off had long been predicted was lying in a bathtub in which ice was melting as fast as it could be replaced.

They rushed in and out of the open front door, left their contributions in the hall and went out for more, though some claimed afterward to have seen me laid out in the tub beneath a mound of ice with nothing showing but my head.

According to Dot Chafe, I was so close to lifeless that I kept sliding down into the ice and water until she got someone to take hold of me beneath the arms.

In a fever vision, I replayed my descent into the gully, which was not nearly as cold or deep as I expected. I splashed around and someone grabbed my wrists and someone else my shins and a man's voice that wasn't Dad's said it would be the end of me if I did not keep still. "The fever's coming down, but he's not out of the woods yet."

Then Lucy said, "Leonard, calm down, we're trying to help you," and she told me to kneel, and someone wondered if the time had come to call the priest. Or was the worst over? "You should have seen him when I got here." That was Dot's voice. "My first thought was the priest. The youngster was shivering like a petrified cat." Not out of the woods. Death warmed over. Boiled over. If he had been any hotter, he would have whistled like a kettle. It was nice to sit beside a fire when your clothes were wet.

When I woke again, I was sitting on the end of Jennie and Dad's bed, propped up by Ken and Craig on either side of me. I looked at myself in the mirror above the dresser. I was wearing pants and socks but no shirt. I looked like a dumbfounded simpleton, eyes drooping, mouth agape, my upper front teeth a jagged series of incisors.

"Just watch, Jennie," Craig said. He and Ken let go of me and I flopped back on the bed. "He can't even *sit* up," Craig said, laughing. "I think he threw up his spine."

Jennie said that I was not a toy. "Put his shirt on," she said. She sat at the dresser, applying lipstick.

My brothers pulled me back up and managed to get me into a shirt. They buttoned it and tucked it in as best they could.

Dad came into the room. "He's going to the hospital," he said.

"He's going to Dr. McIntyre's," Jennie said. "His office is closed, but Dot called him for me."

Dad said what about the ambulance that was on its way. Jennie said it wasn't on its way anymore because Dot had cancelled it.

"He needs to go to the hospital. He almost—"

"He didn't almost do anything he didn't almost do before. He's sick because you took your eye off him and he fell into the gully. He probably swallowed some of that water. God knows what's in it."

Dad said what did it matter *why* I needed to go to the hospital as long as I needed to go.

Jennie said she was not having one of hers go to St. John's in the back of an ambulance with its lights flashing and siren screeching. Dad wondered if she would be mortified if one of hers went to the hospital in a silent ambulance with no lights flashing.

"Ned is driving us to Dr. McIntyre's," Jennie said.

"Watch, Dad," Craig said, and he and Ken let go of me and I flopped back on the bed again. Dad said I should be on a stretcher which, in case she didn't know, lessened a sick person's chance of getting injured while being transported from here to there.

Jennie said she didn't want to hear anything more from the person responsible for having half of Petty Harbour Road traipse through the house as if that was how many people it would take from now on to keep one of hers alive. She said it would be a long time before people stopped talking about what sort of help the Johnstons might need in the future and what ungodly hour they might come looking for it.

Dad stormed out of the room.

"Get his shoes on," Jennie said to Ken and Craig. My shoes were right at my feet. Craig held me by both shoulders as Ken forced my feet into my shoes and tied the laces. I heard Ned's truck pull into the driveway. I knew he wouldn't come in and that Lucy was watching from their front window.

"The two of you are going to help him out to the truck," Jennie said. Craig tousled my hair. Ken patted my chest. It was an adventure for them to help with this nighttime trip to Dr. McIntyre's. They wouldn't have missed it for anything. Everyone who took part in the race for ice would want to know what happened afterward. My brothers would make jokes and exaggerate. I might even get some mileage out of it.

They each put one of my arms around their shoulders and raised me from the bed. They slowly made for the door with me between them, the toes of my shoes dragging on the rug in the hall.

"I think he's asleep again," Craig said and began to laugh just as my hand slid out of his. The other slid out of Ken's and I crumpled to the floor.

"I can't get a good grip on him," Craig said. "His hands are so small and sweaty."

"Where's Dad?" Ken said.

"Sulking in the bathroom is my guess," Jennie said. "Pick Wayne up by the arms and feet and carry him out like that. And don't drop him. Be careful going down the steps."

And so they carried me out to the truck in the manner in which bodies are carried from the battlefield, my backside sometimes brushing the ground.

Many of those who had contributed ice were now flanking the driveway. I saw their legs as I slowly turned my head from side to side.

"Poor soul," a woman said. "I'll say a prayer for him, Jennie."

Poor soul. Just a soul now, not one inside a body anymore. I'd never been able to imagine what heaven would be like. Was I on the way but not yet there?

Some of those standing round helped Ken and Craig hoist me into the back of Ned's truck, where I lay on my back, my head in Craig's lap. I felt empty of all strength and energy, completely indifferent to what would become of me. The thought of being taken to a doctor would ordinarily have had my heart pounding, but when I felt the truck begin to move, I drifted off to sleep more peacefully than I ever had in my life.

ten

I woke, supine and shirtless again, this time on Dr. McIntyre's examination table. Jennie was beside me, holding my hand, her rosary wound tightly round her other fist like a set of brass knuckles.

"He's coming to," the doctor said. "That's a start. But I meant it when I said I'll drive him to the hospital myself if I have to."

"Yes, sir," Jennie said, her tone as flat as if he had asked her if her name was Jennie.

Dr. McIntyre stood on the other side of the table from her. He wore the cleanest, brightest, most perfectly ironed and creased white shirt I had ever seen. But there was a congealed drop of gravy on his tie, and he smelled the way Dad did when he came out to the car from the Crystal. For some reason, I found the spot of gravy more remarkable than the way he smelled.

"Now, Mrs. Johnston," he said, "go out to the waiting room with your other boys."

"I'll sit down over here," Jennie said, taking a chair just inside the door. The doctor said nothing. I was fairly certain that Jennie had picked up on the smell.

"So, young man," the doctor said, in what Jennie later told me was a Scottish accent, "your mum tells me you've had a bad night?"

I nodded.

"Not your first one, by the look of you," he said.

His office was not far from St. Kevin's, but this was my first visit—the first, in fact, by any member of my family. In our world, which I had no reason to think was different from anyone else's, you went to a doctor only on those rare occasions when you suffered a lapse in common sense and brought upon yourself some illness or injury your mother had taught you to avoid. You only needed the stopgap of a doctor to get you back to the point at which she could resume her role as primary physician.

But Jennie also saw doctors as recruiters of patients for hospitals and was even less likely than her peers to entrust anyone, herself included, to their care.

"I need to listen to your heart and lungs," he said. "Your lungs first. Can you sit up?"

I tried but barely managed to raise my head off the exam table.

"Maybe Mum will be useful after all," the doctor said, though he didn't look at her. "Could you help him sit up and keep him from falling off the table?"

"Yes, sir," Jennie said. Firmly but carefully, one hand round the back of my neck, the other gripping my upper arm, he raised me to a sitting position while Jennie held me at the hips.

He pressed the cold stethoscope against my back. "Take a deep breath and slowly let it out," he said. I breathed in but broke into a cough while breathing out. The rattle in my chest was back. I was surprised. I thought I had heaved out of me everything that made it hard for me to breathe.

"You have a cough like someone who's been smoking for forty years," the doctor said. I looked at Jennie, whose eyes were downcast as if she'd been chastised.

"Try again," the doctor said. Same result. It was all Jennie could do to keep me upright.

"How long has he had this cough?" the doctor said.

"Forever," Jennie said. "When we lived in town, a doctor gave us this gizmo to make it better but it didn't work."

"An inhaler," I said.

"He speaks," the doctor said. "Was he diagnosed with asthma?"

"That inhaler made everything worse," Jennie said. "He catches everything that's going around."

"Everything that's been going around has been catching him. No wonder—he's malnourished."

"There's always enough food but he won't eat. I mean, he eats, but beyond a certain point he can't keep it down."

"I think he has pleurisy. Inflamed lungs. When was the last time he had an X-ray?"

"I'm not sure."

"Did the doctor who gave him the *gizmo* prescribe an *X-ray*?" McIntyre said.

"I don't know."

"Well, who would know if *you* wouldn't?" McIntyre said. When Jennie said nothing, the doctor shook his head in dismay. "His teeth are broken and his lip is bleeding. How did *that* happen?"

"He passed out tonight and hit his mouth on the edge of the bathroom sink."

"Is that what happened?" McIntyre asked me.

I nodded.

"How is it that this boy has never been to see me before?"

"We just moved back here from St. John's," Jennie said.

"But you lived here before, didn't you?"

"Yes," Jennie said. McIntyre shook his head again. "He's never been this bad," Jennie said. "I do my best with him."

"Aside from keeping him away from hospitals and doctors."

Jennie looked flustered. "My other three are right as rain. Wayne stays awake all night except he sleeps a bit when he's sitting up. Lying down makes him cough."

I remembered Lucy saying, "They better bury you sitting up or you'll be coughing in your coffin until Judgment Day."

"Christ," McIntyre said. "Let's lie him back down again."

After they did, McIntyre sent Jennie back to her chair. He put two fingers on my belly and tapped them with the same two fingers of the other hand. He did it again and again.

"I'm going to listen to your heart, young man," he said. "Just keep still and breathe as normally as you can. Try not to cough."

He pressed the cold stethoscope against various parts of my upper chest, furrowing his brow and squinting as if he was trying to make out what someone in a crowded room was saying to him. He moved the stethoscope about as if he couldn't find my heart, as if I might not have one or it was darting about faster than he could keep up with it.

He put his face close to mine and I smelled the beer again. He knit his eyebrows in puzzlement as if he had no idea what to do. He stood up straight and, sighing with frustration, put his hands on his hips.

"I'll give him a booster shot," he said at last. He opened a drawer in the exam table and took out a syringe. He glanced at Jennie. "And I'll give *you* some penicillin for him. Not a prescription. I'll give you the pills myself, and you'll make sure he takes them."

"Yes, sir."

He rubbed my upper left arm with a cotton swab soaked in alcohol. "Nothing but bone," he said as he jabbed me with the needle.

My arm felt as it did when I hit my funny bone on something, only along its entire length. A guitar string vibrating silently.

"If that doesn't perk him up, nothing will. Everything in it but the kitchen sink."

He fastened some cotton to the spot with a Band-Aid. "Help me get his shirt back on. Then have your other boys take him to the waiting room. You stay here. I'll get you those pills and we'll have a little chat."

⌘

I sat between Ken and Craig in the otherwise empty waiting room, feeling faintly better, my arms limp at my sides, my head resting against Ken's arm. Ned was outside in the truck.

The doctor's office door was closed. He spoke for a long time, but I couldn't make out a word.

Then Jennie spoke, her voice louder than his, telling him about the doctor who had long ago diagnosed a nervous cough.

"No one has a nervous cough because they're nervous," Dr. McIntyre all but roared. "If that's what the man said, he's incompetent, but we'll never know what he said or what he meant or who he was, because *you* can't recall his name. He might not even exist. A nervous cough. Specialists are not even sure if there *is* such a thing but, if there is, it has to do with the nervous systems of the body, the central nervous system and the autonomic nervous system. If there's something wrong with them, it triggers, or it might trigger, a cough response. Do you understand a word I'm saying?"

"Yes, sir. Some of it. Not all of it as such."

"*Christ.*"

They spoke in low tones again for a while until Dr. McIntyre shouted: "Take him on the goddamn bus if you have to. Just get him there."

Craig grinned at Ken, but Ken looked scared.

I waited for Jennie to rip into the doctor. There was silence for a while. Then Jennie murmured until he interrupted her.

"This is not the goddamn seventeenth century. At least it's not in the rest of the Western world. What's your plan? *Hope* for the best? Light a candle for him? I've worked in Africa and come up against less stubbornness and ignorance. I'll have

Social Services look into this. There'll be a welfare officer on your doorstep before the week is out. Everyone will see the car in your driveway."

He had her number. People would see the car in the driveway. They'd know why it was there. Men, women and children running from house to house, looking for ice in the middle of the night. No child of hers would set foot in an ambulance or hospital. The night the sickly Johnston boy was carried from the house by his brothers. I was the measure of her mothering skills. It struck me that, in her mind, this had always been so, that this was how she had always seen me, as the one of her children by whom she was judged, because of whose unaccountable sickliness and scrawniness and sheer oddness she had earned the reputation she believed she had. She was not, in the eyes of the people of the Goulds, as estimable as I had thought, and this was my fault.

The office door opened. Jennie came out and eased the door shut again. Her face was ashen. She looked like she might start to cry. She walked slowly into the waiting room with a bottle of pills and a piece of paper in her hand. She put the piece of paper in the pocket of her coat, then took it out again and put it and the pills in her purse.

"Come on then, boys," she snapped, looking at the floor. "Help Wayne into the back of the truck, and Ned will drive us home."

The doctor had shouted at Jennie. He had ripped into her. No one in the back of the truck said so. No one in the back of the truck said anything. The three of us sat with our backs to the window of the cab. I was glad I couldn't see the back of

Jennie's head. I knew she was not saying anything to her father about what had happened. She would have smoked a cigarette in front of him, lit one up as she sat beside him in the truck, before she told him that.

I had never heard anyone shout at Jennie the way the doctor had, not even Dad, who always shouted as if he knew he would lose the argument, that he would wind up saying worse things about himself than she was saying, and then would come the old switcheroo, she giving him a pep talk and telling him he was better than he gave himself credit for. But the doctor had ripped into her and Jennie hadn't raised her voice, not even once.

After Ken and Craig helped me down from the truck, I was able to make my way inside, though they flanked me just in case. Perhaps the booster shot was taking effect, or I was being held erect by sheer adrenaline. We followed Jennie into the kitchen, where Dad was sitting, shirtless, at the table, smoking a cigarette.

I was behind Jennie, but I saw Dad's face, which told me that he could tell from the look on *her* face that something had happened. She wouldn't tell him that the doctor had ripped into her, but she would have to tell him something.

She had me wash down a pill with a mouthful of water.

"Go to your room, boys," Jennie said. "Help Wayne with his bed. He's sleeping with the three of you tonight no matter how much noise he makes. And close the bedroom door behind you."

After my brothers helped me out of my clothes and into my pajamas, I lay down on the bedmobile between the two bunkbeds. Ken and Craig climbed under the blankets, but they didn't go to sleep. Brian rolled over but didn't wake up.

Jennie and Dad talked for a long time. I strained to hear what was being said, but all I could make out was Dad murmuring when Jennie gave him time to and then Jennie talking again, her tone insistent. Now and then, she made a kind of hissing sound as if she would have shouted if there was no one in the house but the two of them.

After they finally went to bed, I had a coughing fit. Craig said I had to go. That was fine with me. I opened the door and Ken and Craig silently pushed the bedmobile out to the living room.

I lay on the bed at an angle to the floor. I no longer felt sick, merely empty, even hungry, though I wouldn't have dared to sip from a glass of Quik if it had appeared in front of me.

I spent much of the next day at Lucy's, lying on the angled bed.

"I'm surprised your mother didn't stay home with you after what you went through," Lucy said.

I suspected that Jennie had gone to work so that I couldn't ask her any questions about why Dr. McIntyre had ripped into her.

"I got out of bed when I heard all the commotion across the road," Lucy said. "I phoned three times, but the line was busy. At first, I thought the house was burning down. Then it looked like Halloween, people coming and going with all those containers. I bet there wasn't an ice cube left on Petty Harbour

Road. That must have been strange, taking a bath in a tub full of other people's ice."

"I was asleep, sort of."

"You had a close call, my love. 'Asleep, sort of.' I never saw the like, a whole town pitching in to bring down one person's temperature. It was like the March of Dimes, but it was all for you. And your mouth looks like a jack-o'-lantern. What happened?"

"I fell and hit my teeth on the sink."

"It looks like you tried to take a *bite* out of the sink. Does it hurt?"

"A bit."

"A bit, I'll bet. You have so many things wrong with you, you don't feel a new one anymore. It's just as well you're not the smiley type."

She said that it was too bad that I didn't still have my baby teeth. She said that God gave us baby teeth to practise with. By the time our baby teeth were gone, we were as ready as we'd ever be for the only other set we'd ever have.

Why didn't God make us so that our teeth kept growing back, over and over? I asked.

She told me to stop asking why things were one way and not another way. I was second-guessing God. So what if some things didn't make sense? That was just how it was. It had taken her a lifetime to learn as much as she knew, but I was only seven and already asking enough questions to drive a saint to suicide. She didn't know why men didn't get a second head of hair. She didn't know why, no matter what they did to them, their fingernails kept growing back. On the other hand, no man who had lost his hair had ever shown up on her door-step demanding an explanation for his fingernails. Grown men could accept how things were. Why couldn't I?

We rolled my bed near the table, and then she toasted some bread on top of the stove.

"Where's Murchie?" I said.

"You'll never see that question on a quiz. Where do you think he is? Under the daybed, like always. So, what did the doctor say?"

"I don't know. He gave Jennie some pills for me. And he put a big needle in my arm. A booster shot. To give me a boost. Now my arm feels funny."

"Funny how?"

"Funny-bone funny. Jennie said it will go away."

"Knowing doctors, I wouldn't be surprised if your arm went away. Show me."

I rolled up my sleeve and pointed to the little spot where the needle went in. "It feels funny all the way from my shoulder to the tips of my fingers. I can't lift my arm very far. Hardly at all. I can't move my fingers."

"That's your left arm. You're left-handed. How will you manage?"

I shrugged. "I can't hold a pencil or a fork or the handle of a cup or anything."

She pinched my upper arm.

"Feel that?"

I shook my head. She rubbed the palm of my left hand with her thumb and looked at me. "It just feels buzzy," I said.

"Try to raise your arm."

I raised it about an inch from the bed. "It's hard to get up from lying down, especially if I'm on the floor. I have to roll onto my good side if I'm not already on it."

She shook her head in wonderment. "Did Jennie tell the doctor about your arm?"

"I didn't tell *her* about it until this morning. That doctor shouted at Jennie last night. He said he might call Social Services about me."

"I'd like to see him raise four boys. If you left four boys with him for a day, there wouldn't be much left of him when you got back. Let me see who the patron saint of arms is."

She went to the kitchen counter, opened a drawer, took out a book and, wetting her thumb, flipped through the pages. "Jesus, Mary and Joseph," she said when she stopped. "It's someone named Saint Adrian. When he became a Christian, they cut off his arms before they cut off his head. It's not like being made a saint would cheer you up after that."

After lunch and Ned's nap and no appearance by Murchie, we visited the Shrine.

As we lit the candle, Lucy said, "What do you remember from last night? When people have close calls, they see all kinds of things, especially when they have fevers."

"I heard a lot of noise."

"When Leonard had a fever, he saw my sister, who died when she was his age. He saw other people who died in this house. Whenever he came out of a fever, he described them to a T even though he never set eyes on them."

"I didn't see anyone, but I heard you call me Leonard."

She blessed herself. "Well, that's not a good sign, is it, me calling you Leonard?"

"I didn't *see* you. I just heard you. Is it a bad sign for *me* that you called me Leonard?"

"It might be if the dream was mine, but it was yours." She seemed very upset.

"I didn't see Leonard, Lucy," I said, wishing I hadn't mentioned him.

We were silent for a while. Then I said, "I don't think anyone ever died in our house."

"That house is older than this one. Plenty of people died in it. I knew some of them. The Hennesseys lived there. Died there, too."

"I didn't see them. I didn't see *any* ghosts."

"They're not ghosts. They're called shades. Like shadows. Everyone leaves their shade behind, children especially. But you can't see them except when you're in between this world and the next."

"When you're nearly in heaven."

"No. When you're nearly gone. It might not be to heaven. There's limbo, hell and purgatory, too. Hardly anyone goes straight to heaven. Mary did. She went straight up to heaven through the clouds. That's called the Assumption. She died but she was spared the pain of death, and she wasn't buried, because she never sinned, not once. She didn't even commit original sin."

"Neither did I."

"You did when you were born, and don't ask me to explain. Mary's soul left this world as white as it was when she was born. Your soul is not like that. Yours was spoiled from the start and scuffed a few times after that. Now we'll kneel down and say a prayer for that arm of yours and for everything that's wrong with you. And for all the Hennesseys who died in your house. You're a special boy. They'll appreciate your prayers."

eleven

The booster shot and the pills soon had me feeling better, though not any closer to being healthy than I usually was. When I lay down, my cough was as bad as ever, and nothing looked sufficiently appetizing to inspire me to eat more than a single mouthful.

My arm did not improve. It hung limp at my side like some vestigial appendage. The boy with one numb arm.

Craig said that I was faking it and pinched and prodded my arm until it was bruised all over. I felt the occasional faint sensation but nothing more unless he pressed into bone with his index knuckle, grinding with all his might, which brought on the funny-bone numbness. He continued his experiments on my arm long after he was certain that no one, least of all me, could tolerate the kind of pain I would have felt if I was faking it.

Dad said the doctor must have struck a nerve. No one acknowledged the pun.

Jennie kept saying the problem would go away if we all stopped going on about it. I was certain that, like me, she had smelled the beer on the doctor's breath. But, as the days went by, she made no mention of the doctor, who she must have known had made a mistake with the needle. She couldn't stand to hear anyone talk about my arm. She was embarrassed, ashamed that the doctor had ripped into her and threatened to send a welfare officer to the house. Only people she dismissed as bad families were visited by welfare officers. Parents whose children were forever getting into trouble, skipping school while dressed in rags—children with dirt beneath their fingernails.

I remembered the doctor yelling, "Take him on the goddamn bus if you have to."

She and Dad were already taking the bus to work, every day. What had the doctor been talking about? Take me on the bus where? He would send a welfare officer unless—what? What did she have to do, or else?

Jennie cut up my food. She did it on the kitchen counter, where it was less embarrassing for me. I was just able to manage a fork with my right hand, clasping my fist around it and stabbing at the bite-sized bits of food on my plate.

"Brian did it better than that when he was four," Craig said, as if I had regressed on purpose just to irritate him.

Being unable to hold a spoon, I couldn't eat cereal or soup. Everything dropped back into the bowl before it reached my mouth. Mom said that, for once, my lack of an appetite was paying off. I drank tea by holding the cup with my entire right hand, so I had to let it cool first, even though I liked it hot.

Jennie had to help me on with socks and shoes and she tied my laces.

Craig watched. "He can't even put on his *socks*?"

"It's not his fault," Ken said. He helped me put my pants on, zipped them up and fastened them. Then he tucked the shirt he had just buttoned up into the waistband and looped my belt around me.

I thanked God that I was able to manage in the bathroom. Afterward I would shuffle out with my pants bunched round my feet, then wait in the hall until someone came by to pull them up, zipper them and re-buckle my belt. Brian sometimes did it, or Ken or Jennie or Dad, but never Craig.

"No way am I pulling up his pants," he said.

At the dining room table late at night, after I finished whatever homework I felt like doing with my arm the way it was (I did math in my head and dictated my answers and those related to other subjects to Jennie, who wrote them in my notebook), Jennie would smile at me and ask what they were going to do with me if this or that happened or didn't happen. It bothered me even more than it used to.

Cupping her chin in her hand while she smoked, she'd ask what they would do with me if I didn't grow taller, didn't put on an ounce of weight, stayed as white as a sheet, didn't stop coughing, caught two colds at the same time. What would they do with me if my insomnia got worse and I *never* slept?

I hated it that she wished that they *could* do something with me. I hated when she looked at me as if she was stymied as to how she'd ever get used to having me around.

One night, Craig came out and sat at the table with us. He said that people died from lack of sleep. They got so tired that, finally, they did fall asleep and never woke up.

"I sleep a little bit," I said.

"Your arm sleeps," Craig said. "The rest of you has insomnia. That's how it starts. One arm. Then the other one. One leg. Then the other one. When everything's asleep, you're dead."

"That means *you're* dead every night," I said.

"That kind of sleep is not being dead," he said. "Dead is when a trumpet wouldn't wake you up."

"Craig, stop," Jennie said, but she laughed.

I didn't know why he got such a kick out of scaring me sometimes when, at other times, he was nicer to me than anyone else ever was.

"Craig, stop. Stop making me laugh."

He *could* make Jennie laugh. I couldn't. Dad couldn't. The other boys couldn't. Craig was her favourite son. Not me. I was probably number four. But I was Lucy's favourite grandchild. I was sure of that.

twelve

Christmas that year was a modest affair, not that it had ever been lavish. Our presents consisted of socks stuffed with nuts and grapes, a five-point apple and some hard candy. I kept the candy but gave everything else in my sock to Brian.

Then, in early January, Jennie and Dad came home from work in a large, fin-tailed, late-model Dodge. I was on the chesterfield at Lucy's, watching the road, mystified because the bus had gone by without stopping to let Jennie off, let alone both of them.

When the car turned into our driveway, I thought that this was the welfare officer arriving at last. Then Jennie and Dad got out and headed toward the house, as matter-of-fact as if they had left for work that morning in the car.

"Lucy," I shouted, "Jennie and Dad came home with a *car*."

"It might not be theirs," she said. "I hope it's not. What would they have bought it with?"

The sedan was big, low to the ground, tan-coloured except that one of the back doors was white. It was ours. A Dodge Dart. Two men had taken our other car away, but now we had a car again.

My brothers and I were excited. Craig said they wouldn't have to walk as far to go fishing when Dad didn't have the loan of the Federal Fisheries car. I said that Dad couldn't take me fishing because of my arm. "You'll have to sit in the back seat when he's in the Crystal," Craig said. "Maybe *you* will," I said but he only laughed. From now on, Ken said, Dad and Mom could drive to work and they wouldn't have to wait outdoors for the bus where everyone could see them.

We were even more surprised about the car when Jennie told us she had been let go from her job because she was expecting, even though she was barely showing. What's more, neither she nor Dad looked worried.

Though she wouldn't be going to work, I was to go on spending my days with Lucy. Jennie would have her hands full with looking after my brothers—now that the colder weather was keeping them indoors, they'd be coming home from school at lunchtime and after school was out. She didn't want to overdo it by adding me to her workload, as she was concerned about having another difficult pregnancy—though not concerned enough to put herself under a doctor's care.

"Let go from her job and they buy a car," Lucy said the next day. "What sense does that make?"

It made none, but Jennie was in a better mood for a while.

The six of us went for a drive the first Sunday we had the car, and Jennie bought us ice cream cones. Dad, a cigarette in the fingers of the hand that held the wheel, fiddled with the radio with his other hand. Now and then, Jennie looked into the back seat and smiled at us. "This car is like a late Christmas present for all of us," she said.

Later that month, Jennie said it was time to throw a real party, meaning one for her family. Jennie's brothers and sisters did not come to visit unless she threw a party, and Jennie and Dad didn't go to their parties because, Jennie said, Dad was not a party person. Jennie's parties depended on how big and presentable our current house was. Most of her relatives didn't have cars, so there had been no parties when we lived in St. John's. Despite having its upper storey blocked off, our present house had a big kitchen, which was where the parties happened, though they often overflowed into other rooms.

Uncle John and his wife, Dot, always came, John bringing rabbits he had snared, partridge he had shot, trout bigger than Dad's or Craig's, cod tongues in large white plastic buckets, black blood puddings, white puddings whose ingredients no one seemed to know, all of which Jennie and her sisters set about cooking right away so they'd be ready later in the evening.

John was slim and tall and handsome and somehow made even the oldest clothes he wore look new and custom-made. He had a tattoo on his forearm from when he'd been in the merchant marine. No one could make Jennie laugh like John could, not even Craig. John couldn't sing or play an instrument, but he was a good dancer.

I was a kind of mascot at the parties, usually watching from the kitchen doorway. I liked watching John. Whenever he caught my eye, he winked as if the two of us shared some secret that no one else would understand.

Even though it was Jennie's party, John was in charge. He and Dot brought a group of their friends, one of whom played the accordion and another the fiddle. John shouted out the names of songs and they played them. The food was a scoff and the dancing was a scuff. A scuff and a scoff. Nothing made you hungrier than dancing did. John said that if I took up dancing, I would eat more and get stronger. I told him that one of my arms didn't work. He said I could dance with one arm. It was one-*legged* dancing that was hard.

I knew that John and Dot would be the last to leave, John because he could drink a lot and not get drunk, and Dot because she was driving, though she also drank a lot. John would leave with a drink in his hand, waving and winking at me.

By nine or ten, after my brothers went to bed, the party really got going. There was only the bathroom between the bunk room and the kitchen. When everyone got up dancing, the whole house shook.

Craig came out a few times in his pajamas and said, "For frig's sake, stop making so much noise." But John picked him up in his arms and carried him back to the bunk room every time, winking at me as he returned to the kitchen.

As others danced, Jennie fried up the massive blood puddings on the stove. Even the sound the puddings made as they sizzled made me queasy. So did the smell of the kidney stew and rabbit stew. When the food was ready, the grown-ups would tuck in as if they hadn't eaten in days.

Drinking had the opposite effect on Dad than it had on John. When Dad drank, he retreated into himself, and the company of other people interfered with this. That night he sat as alone with his brooding thoughts as he could be while surrounded by people having a time. He didn't dance or sing along when the others belted out the songs John told his friends to play. Now and then he tried, or pretended to try, especially when Jennie urged him to. He tried to get into the swing of it, tapping his knee with his hand, stamping his foot, shouting strained encouragement to people who ignored him or awkwardly acknowledged him with as much of a smile as they could manage. But he soon fell silent again, draining his glass in a series of gulps, his head tilted back as if he was scrutinizing the ceiling, though his eyes were closed.

I felt sorry for him. When our eyes met, he looked away.

All three of Jennie's brothers were farmers who had a gift for sniffing out standoffishness, self-consciousness, anything that suggested that a person thought themselves to be somehow unique or superior. At another party, I had seen them pick on a man who tried to laugh off what they said but wound up fighting back, which spelled his doom. In the end, he challenged them all to step outside, and they laughed so hard they had to lean on each other to keep from falling down.

Faces burnt by the sun and the wind, big men with glasses in their hands and mischief in their eyes, they were merciless once they got going, standing shoulder to shoulder like some sort of vaudeville act.

For the most part, out of deference to Jennie, they left Dad alone, but that night, perhaps because there were no other likely targets and he looked as if he felt even more out of place than usual, they didn't.

An *agricultural* technologist who worked for the *fisheries* department. How had that happened? He was like a man who trained with the army and worked with the navy.

He had only to tell them who had made him such an arse-backwards, mixed-up, stuck in reverse, pants pulled on over his head, walking contradiction of a man and they would straighten out both him and the other guy in no time flat.

An expert on farming should be helping men like them. They wanted him to teach them what he had learned during his indoor study of their outdoor occupation. They said Jennie told them he hadn't learned much from Rebecca during his time on Sunnybrook Farm, but that didn't mean he couldn't show them how to better grow their crops and milk their cows instead of wasting that advice on fishermen, who, when they saw him coming, were too polite to drown themselves.

Jennie laughed and told them to stop their badness, but Dad took the bait. He told them they knew nothing about the science of farming *or* fishing, nothing about the modern, more efficient methods that he had learned in agricultural college.

Arthurcultural college? Where he worked in a laboratory?

Dad said the proper pronunciation was la*bor*atory; they asked him if he knew what a man*ur*atory was. They gave him a hint. It was a person who was so full of shit he said la*bor*atory.

My uncles kept on him. Jennie, they said, had asked her brothers if every man's test tube was as small as his. They had covered for him and said yes. He didn't have to thank them— the size of his test tube was the least of their worries.

Dad asked them were they not ashamed of how they talked about their sister? They replied: Was he not ashamed of how his wife talked about *him*?

And what was this they'd heard about him not saying the rosary with his family and not going to church anymore because Jennie sent him there one Sunday when it was so cold outside his test tube shrunk to nothing, which wasn't a lot of shrinking as far as his test tube went, which had never been far enough for Jennie, but at least something had been better than the nothing she wasn't getting stuck with now? And no, he shouldn't put on that face of his, because they were only reporting what Jennie had told them when she called them up at all hours and asked if a certain kind of deprivation might be grounds for an annulment.

Dad said he'd only been kidding about church, that he'd been to church every Sunday since he said he'd never go again. They asked him if Jennie had made him back down by refusing to let him put his test tube in her Bunsen burner.

Your *sister*, Dad reminded them, and you bunch don't even know what a Bunsen burner is. He said that he just went to church for show, that the Bible was made up, all of it, for idiots like them.

Who made the world? my uncles asked.

Maybe no one did, my father responded.

The Bible said that God made the world, but Art Johnston thought that "maybe no one did" was a better answer?

Maybe it was.

So, Gerald said, if you came home and there was something on the kitchen table that wasn't there when you left, like a bag of potatoes, wouldn't you think that someone put it there?

Dad said he might.

So a bag of potatoes had to come from somewhere, but the world could come from nowhere.

Maybe.

Dennis said Dad might be the life of the party if he didn't spend it trying to figure out who made the world.

John asked him why we moved so often. Did Dad think that the key to figuring out who made the world was to visit every inch of it?

"You're a credit to your father," Dennis said, "even if you don't know who he was."

He didn't know where the world came from. He didn't know where he came from or how he got to where he was. He didn't know where he was going. Art Johnston in a nutshell.

Dad stood, glass in hand, stormed out of the kitchen to the bedroom and slammed the door.

"Is he gone to *bed*?" Dot said, unable to suppress a laugh.

"I think he's sitting on it," Jennie said, and she also laughed, then flashed a look at me.

For the rest of the night, when Jennie knocked, Dad opened the door just enough to exchange his empty glass for a full one. And whenever she gave him a drink through the crack in the door, her brothers started up again.

"Come out, Art, we were just joking. It was you who made the world, wasn't it? Don't be modest now."

"There's a man out here with his eye on Jennie's dumplings, Art. You better not hide for too long."

"Are you planning to stay in there until the baby of whoever knocked her up is born?"

Hours later, when the last of the guests had gone, John spouting apologies dripping with irony and Dot still unable to keep a straight face, Dad came out of the bedroom to the kitchen and opened a beer.

Why couldn't he enjoy himself? Jennie asked. What a spectacle he had made, running off to the bedroom like a youngster and sulking in there half the night, drinking and smoking by himself. Why couldn't he loosen up like everyone else? He hadn't *mixed* with people, he hadn't talked to them, he hadn't really tried.

Dad said her brothers were yahoos, a word that, in case she didn't know it, hadn't existed until a man as estimable as Jonathan Swift, whom he was sure she and her brothers had never heard of, had made it up.

"*Gulliver's Travels*," Jennie said.

"*They* haven't read it," Dad said.

Jennie insisted that her brothers expected him to give as good as he got and tease them back as good-naturedly as they teased him, but he said there was nothing good-natured about them unless she thought that a swarm of piranha were only kidding when they skinned you to the bone. He said they'd know they outnumbered him if they could count to three, but they were grade-school-dropout yahoos, an opinion he wished he could say was his, but he had borrowed it from everyone who had ever met them.

"There you go!" Jennie said. "Why didn't you say something like that to them?" He took everything so *seriously*. If he was told a joke, he didn't get it, and he didn't know how to tell a joke himself, unless he was holed up by himself in the bedroom, sharing a laugh with his reflection in the dresser mirror. He was always on some other wavelength. Couldn't he put aside his worries for a while, couldn't he forget that he was better educated than her family and give them some credit for having a ton of real-life experience and knowledge that wasn't worthless by a long shot?

She'd been drinking—she almost never drank except at parties—and didn't care that I was watching and listening from the bedmobile in the hall.

As the two of them sat on at the kitchen table, she eventually switched to a coaxing, entreating tone.

He winced at every word but nodded as if he saw the sense in what she was saying and knew that he had room to improve where socializing was concerned and this was something he would work on, he would. And then she fell quiet and focused on the cigarette she held between her fingers.

The longer the silence went on, the sadder the whole house seemed. It was as if Jennie had said more than she intended to and couldn't take it back and neither of them was sure what the implications of this might be for the future. They had dragged into the light something they both knew was best left in the dark. They had done it before, and they would do it again. They only had to wait for it to go back into the dark, and then they would move on for a time until they dragged it back into the light again.

thirteen

A few days after the party, Jennie and I were at the homework table, me doing quadratic equations, which she still referred to as my sums, as she smoked and watched me.

"We're going to the doctor tomorrow," she said.

"You and Dad?" I said, thinking there was something wrong with the baby.

"*You* and Dad and me," she said.

"Dr. *McIntyre*?" I was still mystified as to what she was supposed to do to stave off the welfare officer. It had been two months since my close call, and the only thing different now was that we had a car and she had no job.

"Art is taking the day off and he's driving us to town. It's not a hospital. You won't be staying overnight. It's a clinic in an office building. Dr. McIntyre did refer you, though. That means he sent a note to the new doctor, telling him to expect you."

"What kind of doctor am I going to see?"

"A cardiologist. A heart man. A man shaped like a heart."

I didn't laugh, because the tone of her voice had changed. She sounded nervous.

"What's wrong with my heart?" I said.

"This doctor is going to make sure that nothing is wrong with it."

"But Dr. McIntyre thinks there is?"

She sighed and rubbed her forehead with one finger of the hand that held her cigarette. I saw that she was on the verge of tears.

I remembered Dr. McIntyre examining me with his stethoscope, moving it about ever faster, and also his quizzical, intense expression as he strained to make out the sounds inside my chest. I hadn't dwelt on it much since. Despite my many ailments, perhaps because of them, I never brooded about my health. I'd more or less come to expect that new problems would crop up but that I would somehow learn to live with them and continue on into adulthood in spite of the many grown-ups who openly rated my chances of doing this to be all but non-existent.

That my heart might now be joining the list of my many underachieving body parts did not surprise or distress me. I had only the vaguest notion of what the heart was for and no idea what might be done to it, or for it, that might make me less of a nuisance to everyone. At even the most eventful times, my mind was inclined to jump from one thing to another, given that the world was a place to which I'd never felt entirely attached. Had I, on top of everything else, tended to hypochondria, I might have fretted to death.

Take him on the goddamn bus if you have to.

To take your son to this heart doctor, I now assumed Dr. McIntyre had meant. Jennie must have cited our lack of a car as a reason for *not* going. She'd imagined the three of us conspicuously boarding a bus full of people who would wonder why I was coming with them to town, among them some of those who'd contributed ice to bring down my fever, because the hapless mother, Jennie Johnston, had been unable to take care of her unimprovable son. But now she had a way of getting to town without having to resort to the mortification of a bus. Had they bought a car just to take me to a doctor in St. John's?

Even though I hadn't said a word of what I'd been thinking, Jennie started crying, not just leaking tears but sobbing loudly.

Before I could ask what was wrong, Craig was standing beside me in his pajamas. His feet were bare, and his pajamas, which had once belonged to Ken, were far too big for him, the sleeves covering all of his hands but for the tips of his fingers. He wore the scornful expression that the very sight of me could bring to his face, the one that was mixed with perplexity as to why nothing was the way Jennie deserved it to be.

All but crying himself, he ripped into me.

"Why do you have to be so *out* of it all the time? You never notice *anything*. Why do you think they bought the friggin' car?"

"Now, Craig," Jennie managed to say between sobs. "Don't wake your father."

"Did you think the car was just for you?"

"No," I said, having no idea how he'd guessed that I'd wondered if it was.

"You're about to go to a lot of different doctors," he said. "Too many to go to on the goddamn bus. They're spread all over town. Places that *no* bus ever goes."

"How many doctors?" I said, looking at Jennie, who was wiping her eyes with the back of her hand.

"How many doctors?" Craig said in the squeaky, peevish voice of mimicry. "You have to have a whole once-over. You have *everything* wrong with you. You're like a car that got totalled in a crash. If you don't see the doctors, the welfare will come and take you to some foster home in town. I wouldn't care, except they might take Brian, too, and maybe me and Ken. The four of us in different foster homes because of you and Dad.

"All Dad ever does is spend the rent. The Crystal would be in the hole if not for him. And you're always friggin' sick. Everybody's nerves are shot because of you. Jennie's nerves are shot to pieces. Cough. Cough. Cough. Maybe that's not your fault but it's your fault that you haven't got a clue. Jennie and Dad haven't got a cent, but they bought the car to make a good impression on the welfare. A car in the driveway for when they pass by, because now they have their eye on us, day and night. But how would you know? You're always at Lucy's. And we're not supposed to talk about it in front of you in case you get even sicker."

I started bawling then, and Craig, as usual, pulled me out of my chair and wrapped his arms around me and put his chin on top of my head.

"You're not all that friggin' bad," he said, sniffling himself. "Sometimes you're not. You're pretty good at stuff that no one gives a frig about, like books, right? It's not easy being sick just because someone looks at you sideways. You're not that friggin' bad, right?"

I nodded against his chest.

"We might find out what we were missing if the welfare put you in a home where no one gave a frig about you. You might, too. If all those doctors put their heads together, they might come up with something. They might not fix you but maybe they could give you a tune-up."

I didn't care that he was paraphrasing Dad and Jennie and maybe even Ken. I didn't care that he was hugging me so hard I could barely breathe.

Then Dad came out of the bedroom and sat at the table with us.

"We can afford the car, honey," Jennie said to me. "Without the car, we'd have to take taxis in town. You can't walk very far, especially not in this cold weather. We won't have to pay for taxis or bus fare. We bought the car because it all evens out."

"It *doesn't* even out," Dad said, shifting to get closer to her. "It doesn't nearly even out. It's simple arithmetic. What's wrong with waiting for the bus, being seen waiting for the bus? No one else on the bus has a car, either. But you couldn't be seen with Wayne on a bus. How would that have looked? And walking with him in St. John's? Another scandal, a woman and her son walking in St. John's. And imagine coming home in a *taxi*. The talk would never end."

"I could have asked Ned to let you borrow his truck," Jennie said. "He hardly drives it. But you wouldn't let me because of how *that* would look, driving around St. John's in a stake-bodied farm truck."

"How would I park a thing that size in St. John's? And I've never driven a truck in my life. I might not know how."

"You wouldn't give Lucy or him the satisfaction of asking for a favour."

"That's true. I wouldn't. But I still couldn't manage that truck."

"If you stopped drinking—"

"I have a few beers just like every other man in the Goulds. We both smoke cigarettes. I budget it all out. But you had to have a car, even though you lost your job. And on the weekends I have to cut the hair of every youngster in the Ghouls for twenty-five cents a head, as if anyone but their mothers could care less what they look like."

"If I hadn't lost my job now, I would have lost it when I had to miss work to take Wayne to the doctors. It all evens out."

"Jesus."

I didn't know how much everything they mentioned cost or how much money Dad made, or Jennie used to make. But I knew that few things played more on her mind than the question of how everything she did looked to others. Dad was right about that. And she was right about him spending *some* of the rent, but so did she. Dad had been against getting the car, but he loved to drive it. He washed it and waxed it, not to impress others but out of self-respect and pride, which he paradoxically flouted whenever he went to the Crystal in the car.

Dad went back to bed.

Jennie shouted that he should remember she was pregnant. This was her fifth pregnancy. Five times nine months was forty-five months, minus four months for the one still on the way. Forty-one months. What had he had to do five times to make five youngsters? Nothing that gave you stretch marks. Maybe that was why she didn't want to walk all over St. John's in the winter with a youngster who, for all she knew, she might wind up having to throw over her shoulder. Maybe that was why she didn't want to hop on and off buses. Had he forgotten that, in winter, the sidewalks of St. John's were covered in ice and snow that you could slip on?

How could he forget? he shouted. He *made* those sidewalks slippery. Everything was the way it was because he made it that way. All she had to do was ask her brothers. The whole world was his fault.

Early the next morning, before my brothers set out to walk to school through a cold winter rain, I headed for St. John's with my parents in the Dodge, Dad and Jennie in the front, me feeling very much alone in the big back seat, hugging the passenger door, looking out the window at the wet trees going by, having spent the night wide awake on my bed in the living room—on it, not in it—pretending to read a book, brooding about how Craig had ripped into me and wondering if he had really felt sorry about it or had only pretended to. Maybe he liked to push me to tears because he liked even more the bittersweetness of forgiving me, of pushing *himself* to tears because he had once again forgotten that I couldn't take it, that I was more easily hurt than others and needed his protection.

Now, in the car, I tried to decide if I was as clueless as Craig had said I was, and if the rest of the family agreed with him, or if it was true that I was helpless to resist whatever in God's name it was that made me such a burden on them.

Jennie hadn't slept, either. I had heard her in her room, lighting up one cigarette after another, three clicks of the lighter for every smoke. Several times, on the way to the bathroom, I'd snuck a glance through the crack of the bedroom door and had just been able to make her out, one hand behind her head as she blew smoke toward the ceiling.

She, too, looked out the car window at the woods she had never ventured into in her life, the dark mid-winter spruce bowing in the wind that slammed the car. I guessed she was talked out from the night before. Though Dad hadn't been drinking last night, he seemed to be deep in the misery and reverie of a hangover.

After he parked outside the heart doctor's office, Dad said he would wait for us in the car. Jennie didn't protest, just gave him a look that said he'd better be here when we came back out.

The waiting room had the look of a judge's chambers, with its wainscotted walls and brown leather chairs and green desk lamps, from which gleaming chains hung down. Everything looked fancy, newly polished and expensive. It was empty of patients but for us. There was a No Smoking sign on one of the coffee tables. Jennie wouldn't have smoked in a place like that even if it wasn't forbidden.

A nurse receptionist with her hair pinned in a perfect blonde bun showed us to the doctor's office. His name, Dr. Philip Barton, underscored by his credentials in initials, was on a door that had no window.

"Mind your manners," Jennie whispered. I was dressed in my Sunday best, which consisted of my school uniform, which I doubted I would ever grow out of. I pictured myself still wearing it when I was Jennie's age.

We sat side by side on swivel chairs across from a middle-aged white-haired man in a pristine lab coat. A specialist. I'd never seen Jennie so nervous. Her hands shook in a way that a cigarette would not have stopped.

Dr. Barton didn't seem put off by how I looked. He gave the impression that he already knew exactly what was wrong with me and how to fix it. In a surprisingly gentle voice, he informed me that, before he examined me and carried out some procedures, he was going to ask me a number of questions that Jennie was not to help me answer.

"Yes, sir, of course," Jennie said as if she had been instructed by a doctor to keep silent many times before. The doctor smiled at her as if she had said something that he found charming. She smiled back.

Despite her aversion to doctors, I had heard her say of an occasional one that he was a "great man." To her, this meant that, if ever there was someone whose credentials, accomplishments and social standing entitled them to put on airs, this man was it, and yet he had done just the opposite. He had made her feel at ease, made it clear that he truly cared and had acted as if he had grown up just as she had. I felt certain that she was going to tell Dad that this heart doctor was a great man.

Dr. Barton asked me if I had ever had chest pain, back pain, shortness of breath, rapid heartbeat, irregular heartbeat, coughing fits, a burning sensation in my throat, nausea, pain in my left ear but not my right, pain in my left jaw, left arm or hand, night sweats, lack of appetite, stomach pain, difficulty going to the bathroom. He went on and on and I became ever more anxious because I was answering yes to every question. He looked as if he wasn't at all surprised that he was correctly guessing every complaint I had ever had.

"Now, Mrs. Johnston," he said, "I'll carry out those procedures I mentioned."

"Yes, doctor," Jennie said, as if the carrying out of procedures was the obvious next step to her as well. But then he asked me one more question.

"Have you ever heard a hissing sound from inside your chest, a sound like air escaping from a tire?"

"No," I said.

"You're sure."

"Yes."

"Mrs. Johnston?"

"A hissing sound?"

"Yes."

"Not as such."

"But a sound *something* like that?"

"Not as such. No. Well, no. I'm not sure. When he's been coughing for a long time, there's no telling what kind of sound his chest might make. It's hard to tell one sound from another."

He nodded and wrote something down.

"We'll go into my exam room now," he said.

"Yes, sir," Jennie said.

"Just Wayne and me."

"Yes, sir," Jennie said again, as if she was well used to parting company with me at just this point in the carrying out of a cardiological examination.

Dr. Barton seemed not even faintly interested in the story of how my arm had come to be immovable. When I began to recount the trip to Dr. McIntyre's in his exam room, he ignored me. But he gave me a boost up onto the table and he helped me off with my blazer and shirt and tie as briskly and efficiently as if it was in the undressing of boys with one bad arm that he was chiefly trained.

I was able to sit up on the exam table without assistance and was surprised that, at the sight of his sphygmomanometer and his stethoscope, I didn't burst into a fit of coughing.

He took my blood pressure, looking poker-faced at the dial. Then he examined my back and chest with his stethoscope. Throughout, he kept nodding slightly.

When he was done, he said, "I'll need to take a few X-rays. No one told you to wear running shorts and shoes?" I shook my head.

He had me remove my shoes, socks, shirt and school slacks, then showed me to a small room down the hall in which there was a dark, closet-like compartment with supports to keep my arms at shoulder height—he lifted my bad arm and moved it about until it was situated to his satisfaction. He left the little room and closed the door.

"Now, Wayne, I want you to keep completely still until I tell you otherwise."

There was a series of loud sounds all around me, shunting, whirring, clanking. A giant robot triggered into action.

He opened the door, lifted my arm off the support and led me out and down the hall to another room with another such compartment, except that this one had no arm supports. He had me go inside and face away from him, staring at a blank wall.

"When I tell you to," he said, "I want you to start running on the spot. Just move your legs up and down as best you can."

He left the compartment and closed the door. Soon after, he called, "All right, Wayne, start running."

I began to run in place, very slowly, unable to remember when I had last run for more than a few seconds.

"Faster, please, Wayne," he said. "The faster you can go, the better."

I ran faster, lifted my knees higher, pumped my good arm while the other swayed back and forth, limp, useless. When I began to cough, I slowed down.

"It's all right if you cough," he said. "In fact, it's better if you do. Just keep running. I *need* to see what everything looks like when you're coughing. I know it's hard, but if you get sick, you'll have to come back and do this all over again a month from now, so try your hardest not to get sick."

As the coughing got worse, he told me to run faster still. I did as best I could. Sweat dripped from my forehead, into my eyes, down my cheeks and onto my lips and chin. My breastbone felt as if it was about to break, and a scorching pain began to rise in my throat.

"Just a little faster for a little longer," he called. "Don't get sick."

I managed to speed up slightly. I was no longer coughing, just rasping. I couldn't hear my feet hitting the floor.

Just as my legs gave way beneath me, I heard him say, "Well done." I fell on my bad side, my good arm clutching my heaving stomach.

"Your face is as red as a beet," Jennie said when the doctor had the nurse call her in from the waiting room. "And you're soaking wet."

I was dressed, still out of breath, and in the midst of what I knew would be an epic fit of coughing.

"I'm fairly certain he has pleurisy," Dr. Barton said as he and Jennie sat on opposite sides of his desk. "It's treatable but almost certain to recur, judging by the scar tissue on his lungs. But your pulmonologist, your lung man, will tell you more about that. There may be some other things he'll want to

rule out. Wayne has chronic malnutrition and various associ-
ated vitamin deficiencies. Possibly some other issues. Maybe a
tapeworm. There are a lot of maybes where Wayne is concerned. Your gastroenterologist will address some of those.
Same thing with his arm and your neurologist. Dr. McIntyre's
not to blame. This kind of injury to a nerve in the arm from a
needle is a fluke, a one-in-a-million thing. The nerve usually
heals with the help of a physiotherapist.

"*My* biggest concern is that he has a heart murmur. Quite
pronounced. It means—it may mean—that the blood is not
moving properly through the chambers of his heart."

He said that the murmur might be benign—most were—
but he wasn't sure about this one and felt that he should send
my file and X-rays to a heart man in Montreal, more or less
a heart murmur specialist. He said that it was possible that a
trip to Montreal for surgery would be necessary as soon as
possible, since malignant murmurs became more difficult to
repair as the patient got older. He repeated that the murmur
might be benign but he wanted to rule out malignancy.

"Yes, sir," Jennie said. She was trying hard not to cry.

"It's a lot to take in all at once, isn't it? But Wayne is in no
immediate danger."

"Yes, sir."

"It's best that children know the whole story," the doctor
said, looking tenderly at me in a way that made me think he
already suspected the worst and was *withholding* the whole
story, whatever it was.

Dad was asleep in the car when we went out, and woke with a start when Jennie opened the front door. I got in the back.

Jennie told him a very abbreviated version of what the doctor had said.

"Montreal?" Dad cast a glance at me over the back seat. "*Jesus Christ*, we can't afford that, Jen—"

She must have flashed him some sort of look because he fell silent.

As we headed for home, Jennie told Dad what a great man the cardiologist was. Dad nodded as if he was well able to imagine how estimable and learned the man was who had posed them the insoluble problem of finding the money to pay for an extended trip for two or three to Montreal.

Jennie lit a cigarette, her hands shaking.

She asked me to tell Dad what the cardiologist had made me do. When I told him of running on the spot in the dark closet with one arm pumping like a sprinter's and the other swaying lifelessly back and forth, they both laughed.

Dad said I had probably run so fast that my heels had left two permanent dents in my arse. Jennie laughed harder and I stopped coughing.

"The exercise did you good," Dad said.

I knew, then, that Jennie would say yes if I asked if we could stop for wings and chips at a takeout in Kilbride.

I ate a cardboard boat full of wings, chips, dressing and gravy. Dad and Jennie didn't seem upset when, in a gas station washroom a mile down the road, I brought it all back up again.

∾

At home, when everyone was gathered round the table for dinner, Dad had me tell the story of running in the closet, but I didn't tell it as well this time, so it didn't seem all that funny to my brothers.

Jennie told the boys I had what was called a heart murmur, for which I might need an operation in Montreal. The three of them greeted this news solemnly.

After dinner, the boys took turns trying to hear my heart murmur, pressing their ears against my chest and complaining when I coughed that they couldn't even hear the *beating* of my heart. They listened to each other's hearts. "Murmur-murmur-murmur-murmur," Craig said, his ear pressed to Ken's chest. He said that maybe all four of us needed murmur surgery.

My cough grew so bad no one could hear the TV. Craig said they should wheel my bed into the bunk room and close the door behind me.

"Craig!" Jennie said, which meant: if ever there was a night that you shouldn't be mean to Wayne, this is it.

Jennie checked my forehead to see if I had a fever. Craig wondered how a murmur could cause a fever. Ken said the murmur might be the cause of everything that was wrong with me. Jennie said the doctor didn't say that. Dad said I was coughing so much because I had done more running that day than I had done in my entire life. As long as we don't have to go out begging for ice again, Craig said.

"At least he didn't give you another booster shot," Ken said. "He might have double-paralyzed your arm or paralyzed your other one. Then what would you do?" He said I'd have to have my hands tied behind my back to keep my arms from swinging about or just hanging dead in front of me.

Jennie said the doctor said my arm wasn't paralyzed, it was just that the nerve was damaged. It was a fluke, a one-in-a-million thing that wasn't McIntyre's fault.

Dad said the cardiologist was covering for McIntyre. He bet the neurologist would cover for him, too. That was how it worked. Doctors covered for each other. *You make up an excuse for my mistake, and I'll make one up for yours.* That was why the heart man was sending Wayne's file to another heart man. Each one would cover for the other if anything went wrong.

"Art!" Jennie said. Dad said medicine wasn't a real science like math and physics. It was glorified guesswork. But you couldn't beat the pay. Doctors were just quacks who got rich off of poor people.

Jennie said they hadn't paid the doctor a cent, and Dad said where did she think their taxes went?

Dad had changed his tune, Jennie said. Why was he always criticizing her for trying to keep us clear of hospitals and ambulances, never mind doctors? Dad said it wasn't till something really hit home that you saw the truth. And his criticism of doctors was based on evidence, not superstition.

I said the doctor thought that I might have a tapeworm, but that was one for the stomach man.

A tapeworm? Dad said to Jennie. She hadn't told him that.

Jennie said the doctor talked about so many other doctors and about so many things that might be wrong with me, she couldn't keep track. She asked Dad why he hadn't come into the doctor's office. Did he think he had to guard the Dodge because so many thieves were lining up to steal a car with three brown doors and one white one?

"What's a tapeworm?" I asked.

Craig said that it was like a night crawler, only twenty times as big. It lived in your stomach and ate all your food. It was a freeloader. It got a free ride. Room and board until you croaked. Then *it* died, too. You could only get rid of it by putting a piece of pork on a stick and putting the stick down in your stomach, then pulling the stick out bit by bit until you fooled the tapeworm into sticking its head out of your mouth. Then you grabbed it and pulled it up and out like a rope. He said that maybe I coughed so much because I had a tapeworm stuck in my throat, not a frog like other people did. That would be just like me, to outdo a frog with a worm long enough to stretch between two telephone poles.

I asked how you got a tapeworm.

Dad said by eating undercooked meat, or low-grade, improperly stored meat, or by not washing your hands after you used the bathroom. He said it was mostly poor people who got them, ones who didn't know how to handle and prepare food.

Jennie said that, when it came to food, she did the best she could with the small percentage of what Dad earned that made its way into the house and not into the till at the Crystal.

Dad said she bought even cheaper food than they could afford. Even Wayne's tapeworm would turn up its nose at what she was feeding Wayne.

He asked her to consider the Hub. Every two weeks, she

bought a huge wax-encased tube of locally made bologna that bore the brand name Hub. He said that bologna was to steak as the Hub was to the best bologna, which was Maple Leaf. He said that Hub bologna was made with what was left over after real bologna was made, from things that were deemed to be unfit for inclusion in bologna. Food-wise, it was on the lowest rung of the lowest ladder, the bologna ladder, whose first three steps were underground. Hub wouldn't even stay in one piece if it wasn't for the wax.

Jennie said that, pound for pound, it was the best buy you could find. Dad said that was a good argument for buying and serving cow manure. If she bought half as much Maple Leaf bologna, we would eat it all, and it would cost the same as a full tube of the Hub.

Jennie said she didn't want to spoil the boys with expensive food. The most expensive bologna was not expensive, Dad said. Jennie said that if the boys got a taste for expensive food, they would want more of it.

He said that, twice a month, she threw out the Hub. What was the point of that?

She said she would keep buying it and keep throwing it out until the boys ate it all. There was a principle involved, a lesson we would all do well to learn.

He said that we should have a bimonthly ceremony to mark the removal of the old Hub and the installation of the new. This was the hub of his argument.

Jennie said Ha-a and asked him if he had considered the possibility that, if I had a tapeworm, it was because I rarely ate the Hub.

Dad said that he was giving up trying to talk sense into her and went to bed.

Jennie stayed up with me, holding my hand until my cough quieted down enough to allow me to do my homework.

After she finally went to bed, I lay awake, thinking about the possibility that there was a twenty-foot tapeworm writhing around inside of me, and remembering the green liquid I had thrown up on the night of my close call.

I knew why Dad had stayed in the car when we went into the doctor's office. As much as he extolled the scientific view of things, he couldn't stand to be in the company of men he thought were his superiors. He would have been as cowed and deferential as Jennie had been, excruciatingly aware of how much lower he stood on the ladder of science than a cardiologist, who would explain things to him in the kind of layman's terms he had used with us, who could not possibly have understood that he, Art Johnston, might, but for the circumstances of his birth, have risen to just such a place in the world as the man to whom he had brought his son in search of help.

fourteen

Every other day for the next couple of weeks, we drove to St. John's to see specialists. Dad always stayed in the car.

The lung man, Dr. Yap, winced when he first laid eyes on me and said he wasn't certain about the heart man's diagnosis of pleurisy. He wanted to rule out pulmonary fibrosis, which was *very* serious, but he wouldn't know if I had it without performing more X-rays and some blood tests. Like the heart man, he thought it best that nothing be withheld from children, for it was his experience that they would fret more if they were kept in the dark, which made me think of literally being penned up alone in some dark and silent place.

Dr. Yap was younger and of Japanese origin, and his office was not as well appointed as the heart doctor's had been. He X-rayed my chest but didn't make me run. He said that, even while listening to my lungs, he could hear my heart murmur. "Like a murmuring brook," he said. His English was heavily accented, and he frowned when he said "murmur," as if he knew he was mispronouncing it.

He looked down my throat with a light he held in one hand. Another light was strapped to his forehead. He shook his head a lot, as if he couldn't credit what the lights revealed. I wondered how far down inside of me he could see. I asked him if he thought I had a tapeworm, but he didn't answer.

"Three broken teeth," he said to Jennie. "How did this happen?"

"No one hit him or anything like that," Jennie said. "He was so sick he fell and cracked his teeth on the bathroom sink."

The doctor said that fixing my teeth would be too big a job for a dentist. I would have to see an endodontist.

"Yes, sir," Jennie said.

When the examination was complete, Dr. Yap sent me to the waiting room so that he could speak with Jennie alone, which meant that now he *did* want to keep things from me, which must mean that those things were especially bad.

Jennie was in there for fifteen minutes. When she came out, she looked the way she had when she came out of Dr. McIntyre's office. We went out to the little parking lot where, once again, Dad was asleep in the car, his head tilted back against the seat. Again, he woke with a start when Jennie opened the door. She slammed it shut behind her as I got into the back seat.

"What did the doctor say?" I asked Jennie, having already asked her three times and gotten no reply.

"He gave me a note for the next doctor. I don't know what it says. He licked the envelope and closed it. It's a very long note. He wrote the whole thing while I sat there. I could have typed it in two minutes. Why would a lung man have so much to say to a nerve man?" And then she said the lung man had asked if it had occurred to her that living with two heavy smokers might be making my cough worse. Cigarette smoke aggravated every illness he suspected me of having, including pleurisy. He told her to quit smoking and tell her husband to quit, too. He said that I had the lungs of someone who'd been smoking for years. He was certain that all her children did. He said it was a wonder that all *six* of us didn't lie around coughing all night. Then he gave her a prescription for the pleurisy he wasn't sure I had because it would take time to rule out pulmonary fibrosis.

I told Dad that the doctor had said that pulmonary fibrosis was *very* serious. Jennie said that, once it was ruled out, it wasn't serious at all. But she wiped tears from her eyes, and no one said anything else for a long time.

Then Jennie said that when she told the doctor she and her husband didn't have drug insurance, he said the drugs would cost about the same as ten packages of cigarettes or a case of beer. She said she had only told Dr. Yap about the cigarettes. He must have made a wild guess about the beer.

The neurologist, Dr. Peddle, X-rayed my arm and moved it about every which way. He pressed his thumb hard against my funny bone, asked me to squeeze his hand as tightly as I could.

"Your good hand is not much stronger than your bad one," he said as if he was rebuking me for something. "Your upper arm is as thin as your wrist. It's a wonder Dr. McIntyre was able to find a vein. You should be getting proper food and proper rest."

Jennie said I had trouble keeping anything down and my cough kept me awake. "I might have a tapeworm," I said. Peddle nodded as if a tapeworm would be further proof that I was the epitome of neglect. He shook his head.

When Jennie asked, "What did the lung man write to you?" Peddle ignored her. He said that the booster shot had grazed my ulnar nerve. With the help of a physiotherapist, it might heal in a year or two.

"Yes, sir," Jennie said.

He sent Jennie away with another sealed note, this one for the gastroenterologist.

"Why can't they call each other on the phone?" Jennie said when we got back in the car. "Why am I always delivering letters?"

Dad said that they kept copies of the letters for their files.

"Well, what are they writing to each other about?"

"About us," Dad said.

"About Wayne and me," Jennie said. "None of the doctors have ever set eyes on *you*."

Dad said that they were drawing conclusions about him based on us. Jennie said maybe they were drawing pictures of him based on us, and that was what was in the envelopes.

Another X-ray at the stomach man's office. His name was Dr. Hayward. A nurse took blood from my left arm, the one

Dr. McIntyre had jabbed with the booster shot. This doctor was the oldest of them all. He had a pronounced stoop and shuffled along in what appeared to be slippers.

He measured me and weighed me and asked if I was bringing my food back up on purpose. I said no.

"Some children do," he said, adding that my problem might be psychiatric in nature, though the conditions in which I was being raised and the things I was being allowed to get away with, such as staying up all night, not going to school and so on, were doubtless contributing factors.

"So you feel tired all the time?"

I nodded.

"But even when you're not coughing, you can't sleep?"

I nodded again.

"Why not? Is it noisy in your house? Are you afraid of something in your house?"

I shook my head.

I asked him if I had a tapeworm.

He said, "I'll have to do some tests. But children with tapeworms sleep a lot, and tapeworms don't break your teeth."

"The sink broke my teeth," I said.

He wanted a stool sample from me, but I couldn't make myself go, so he gave Jennie a small plastic bag in which, he said, I was to place a sample and then she could bring it back to him.

"First it was letters and now it's Wayne's poo," Jennie said when we got in the car. "What will I be delivering next? Aside from a baby in about three months."

Dad said she'd be having it, not delivering it, which yet another doctor would do.

"He said Wayne's problems might be psychiatric," Jennie said.

Dad said I didn't have a psychiatric heart murmur or psychiatric pleurisy or psychiatric pulmonary fibrosis.

And I wouldn't be having psychiatric surgery in Montreal, Jennie said. It was the stomach man who should have his head examined.

She and Dad laughed a little bit. Then Jennie began to cry again.

A week after Jennie and Dad drove to the gastroenterologist's office and dropped off my sample, we were back there again. Jennie and I sat across from him. He leaned his arms on his desk and hunched so far over it that his face wasn't far from Jennie's.

He said that he was 99 percent sure that I didn't have a tapeworm. He said that it used to be the case that you could only be 100 percent sure by accessing the interior of the body with a pair of scopes, one inserted into the stomach by way of the mouth, the other into the intestines by way of the backside.

"Yes, sir," Jennie said.

He asked her if she understood what he had just said.

"Yes, sir," she answered.

I didn't. I thought he had just told her that he might have to scope out my insides to find a worm that hid so well it couldn't be discovered by any other means.

"So, we will assume that Wayne *does* have a tapeworm and

give him a prescription for medicine to get rid of it. You take it like cough syrup for a couple of weeks. It's expensive. If his symptoms improve, we'll know he had a tapeworm. If they do not, we'll know he didn't." He smiled.

"Yes, sir."

"It is often the conditions in which children live that cause them to develop tapeworms."

"Yes, sir."

"Do you understand what I am saying, Mrs. Johnston?"

"Yes, sir."

"Is your husband waiting outside?"

"Yes, sir. To drive us home."

"Perhaps I could speak to him."

"He's not outside just now. He's picking up some things at work. We're going to meet him down the street."

"Very well. My point is that, unless the conditions I spoke of change, Wayne may get another tapeworm, or he will get one for the first time, as may your other children."

"Yes, sir."

"Do you have insurance for drugs, such as Blue Shield?"

"Not as such," Jennie said.

"Not as such," he said and smiled. "You've seen a lot of doctors recently, and many of them have prescribed drugs for Wayne. One has prescribed physiotherapy. And then there is the possibility that Wayne will have to go to Montreal for open-heart surgery and you will have to go with him. Other things are possible. Have you thought about how you will pay for all of these things?"

"Not as such, no."

He opened a drawer in his desk and pulled out a large manila envelope. "There are some information forms in here, as well as some application forms. All from Social Services. There is also the phone number of a social worker who will help you do what's best for Wayne and you and your family." He extended the envelope to her.

"Yes, sir," Jennie said, taking it from him with both hands.

We walked down the stairs and out the door, Jennie expressionless, holding the envelope in one hand, her purse in the other. Just outside the door there was a garbage can with a swinging lid. Jennie dropped the envelope into the garbage can from about two feet above it.

"Jennie!" I said.

She strode to the car, her heels clicking loudly. I ran ahead of her and was in the back seat by the time she opened the passenger side door. Dad sat up straight and started the car.

"Jennie threw something in the garbage," I said.

"What?" he said, lighting a cigarette.

Jennie got in and slammed the door.

"The only thing that doctor knows how to do is make people feel small," she said, staring at the windshield.

"What did you throw in the garbage?" Dad said.

"Welfare applications—forms for getting welfare to pay for drugs that Wayne probably doesn't even need. It's a money-making racket, prescribing drugs that people don't even need and can't afford."

"The stomach man gave you welfare forms?"

"They're all in on it," she said. "All the doctors we've been to see. He knows about every drug they prescribed. He knows about the trip to Montreal for murmur surgery, which probably won't happen. He knows the lung man is ruling out that fibrosis disease. He said that, most likely, Wayne doesn't have a tapeworm, but he prescribed drugs to get rid of one just in case. Everything is just in case, and second opinions, and ruling out what isn't even there. Two years of physiotherapy for his arm even though the nerve was only grazed. If it will get better just as fast on its own, they can still say it was the physiotherapy that fixed it. If he scratched his head for two years, the nerve would get better. Would that mean that he fixed his arm by scratching his head?"

"Did the doctor say how much everything will cost?"

She said that none of this was that man's business. He was a stomach man, but he wanted to play psychiatrist. What was he going to do, psychiatrize my stomach? Then he wanted to talk to Dad because he didn't think she understood a word he said. She should have told him Dad was snoring in the car. Why were all these doctors ganging up on her, writing each other letters about the conditions Wayne was living in and having her deliver them? They should see what those conditions were doing for her other boys. Did they think her boys were all like Wayne? Did they think the Goulds took up an ice collection every night for one of Jennie Johnston's boys?

"We'll have to do *something* if Wayne has to go to Montreal," Dad said.

"We're not taking a cent from welfare. No Everard ever has, and I won't be the first."

"Well, we're not borrowing any more money."

"We're not doing anything, because the only thing Wayne has is pleurisy, which I never even heard of until just the other day."

Dad said you didn't need to have heard of a disease to get it. Diseases didn't introduce themselves and ask if they could make you sick.

"Really? I thought they were just being uppity with me."

"What about the scopes?" I said.

"What scopes?" Dad wanted to know.

Jennie told him and he said, "Jesus," and looked at me as if to gauge how even one scope, let alone two, would possibly fit inside me. A scope down my throat, which was itself as narrow as a scope. A microscope up my micro-arse.

Jennie laughed, then started to cry.

"We're not going on welfare," she said. "You have a job. I'll have one again, soon enough."

"After you have another youngster we'll have to support."

She didn't reply.

"So," Dad said, "what are we supposed to do? Hoping for the best wouldn't cure Wayne of anything."

"Praying might," she said.

"What has spending half the day in front of Lucy's Shrine got Wayne?"

Wayne might be worse if not for Lucy, Jennie insisted. And speaking of Lucy, she could get the money for the prescriptions from her and they would pay back every cent, like they always did.

"Another loan from Lucy," Dad said. "Jesus Christ."

"It's better than a handout from welfare. It's better than having some stranger size up how good we are at being parents."

"What will happen if you don't call the social worker the doctor told you to call?"

"The same that will happen when *you* don't. Nothing."

"And what about McIntyre, who referred Wayne to all those doctors in the first place? What if he's been keeping in touch with them? You're the one worried about a car from Social Services turning up in the driveway."

"And I suppose you're not."

I felt stricken with guilt about the state the two of them were in because of me. But I resented Jennie for unfavourably comparing me to my brothers right in front of me. I thought about the two scopes the stomach doctor had mentioned even though I didn't need to have them done. Why *had* he told us about them? I imagined being skewered from both ends and the two scopes meeting in the middle, where the tapeworm would be waiting like a third scope whose friends had come to visit.

Since Jennie made me swear not to tell Lucy that she was going to ask her for a loan, I didn't, but I told her about everything else while we were playing cards the next day.

"Your parents should sue that McIntyre man," she said. "A doctor who can't do any better than the Goulds can't be very good. Anyone who comes over here from Scotland is on the run from something. He might as well have lopped your arm right off for all the good it is to you now. An empty sleeve would be better. Lighter. Easier than having to carry a dead arm around all day."

"My arm isn't dead, just asleep."

"A booster shot is what it needs *now*. Mind you, it's not like the first one turned you into a ball of energy. If you have a tapeworm, he picked the wrong place to set up shop. You couldn't bait a hook with any worm that could make its living off of you."

I told her about the heart doctor who made me run on the spot.

"Show me," she said. I did.

She shook her head. "What good was that supposed to do, making you run like that inside a box? It's a wonder your parents didn't bring you *home* in a box."

"I was so tired I fell down."

"And he said you had what? A murmur?"

"Yes. My heart makes a noise."

"Everyone's heart makes a noise. It's when the noise stops that you have a problem. A murmur. It's all made up. Like a rumour. They have to tell you *something*, I suppose."

I told her about the Japanese doctor who said I had pleurisy.

"What's that—a fancy way of saying you can't stop coughing? I hope he didn't come all the way from Japan, not that I know where that is, to give you the news. If he was any good, he'd still be Japanese. Newfoundland is full of doctors from somewhere else. Someone must have put out the word that we'll fall for anything. By the time they get here, they've worn out their welcome everywhere else. I wonder where the good ones go. Once you start with doctors it never stops. They pass you around until you come back to the first one, and then it starts all over again."

I told her the lung doctor was ruling out pulmonary fibrosis. She said it wasn't hard to rule something out. Just from looking at me, she could rule out my being six feet tall.

"I don't think I explained everything right," I said. "I might have got some things mixed up. Sometimes they sent me to another room when they talked to Jennie, and then she wouldn't tell me what they said."

"They've got the living daylights scared out of you," Lucy said. "You can spare those, but doctors have been lopping off parts of you since you were born: tonsils, adenoids, appendix, all before you were five. If that arm doesn't come to life soon, it'll be the next to go. By the time they're finished, there'll be nothing left of you except your clothes. I'll call Luke Joyce and ask him to say a prayer for you. I don't call him very often, because if he says too many prayers, he'll wear out his pull with God. Go take a peek at Murchie, and then we'll go in and say a prayer at the Shrine and you can have some chocolate Quik."

I went to the daybed, used my good hand to lift the blanket and then my good arm as a prop as I bent to look beneath the daybed. Murchie was wide awake, looking as if he'd been cornered and was about to strike back.

"Hello, Murchie," I said nevertheless. He blinked twice and closed his eyes.

At night, my mind swarmed with images and sounds, especially when I was in that state that was the nearest thing to sleep I ever came. I heard, not a murmuring brook, but the gushing of a swollen stream that Dad was trying to carry me across as my heart, in a bid for freedom, rammed against the walls of my chest. I saw the intestines in my textbook illustration of the human body, a mass of tapeworms coiling about in my belly. My numb arm buzzed and vibrated until all of me had that funny-bone feeling. I heard, magnified tenfold, the sound of continuous coughing, felt an unbearable, smothering warmth, sweat stinging my eyes and tasting salty on my lips. I shook, trembled and twitched with cold, waking up on my bed with my sheets and blankets and even my mattress drenched in sweat.

fifteen

Some nights in early February, it was mild enough that Jennie and I could sit on the front steps and watch the traffic come and go on Petty Harbour Road. I sat between her legs, her chin resting on my head, while she puffed on a cigarette.

"This is as far as I will ever get," she said, "living in a house across the road from the one that I grew up in." She said it so often it was like a mantra designed to keep her most dreaded fear from coming true. Often, her face took on a wistful, worried look, as if she was waiting for someone whose return home was long overdue.

Sometimes, depending not only on the weather but on how slippery it was underfoot, we went out for a walk late at night. Dad had made me a kind of staff by sawing my bamboo fishing pole in two—being unable to use one of my arms was affecting my balance, and Jennie was worried that with no way to break my fall, I would trip and go face-first into the ground. Craig said that, when I walked round with my half-length stick of bamboo, which was still taller than me, I looked like Moses.

One night, clutching the bamboo cane in one hand and holding Jennie's hand with the other, I went out for a walk with her not long before the sun came up. We kept our voices down so as not to wake the dogs and, by setting them to barking, wake the neighbours.

We went down Petty Harbour Road, then turned right onto Forest Pond Road and walked around the pond—it was about a mile—looking at the circles on the water made by the occasional trout that was breaching early. Any other year, the pond would have been frozen. Frogs moved among what lily pads were still left on the surface. There was rarely a car, but when one did go by, its driver waved to us.

Jennie never passed a house we had lived in without pointing it out to me, no matter how many times she had done so before.

"We lived there for a while," she said, aiming her cigarette at a house just below the woods on the side of a hill. "It was a nightmare in the winter, going up and down that lane in the car. It's a wonder we didn't all perish in a crash. It was a rough winter, not like this one. We must have had the driveway plowed twenty times because it was too long to shovel out."

She indicated a bungalow at road level.

"Remember living there?" she said.

I shook my head.

"Well, we did," she said, "for four or five weeks after Brian was born. The wind blew right through it. We burned peat moss in the fireplace. The peat smelled nice, but it didn't heat the house very well, so I made these things out of old blankets to keep drafts from coming in beneath the doors. Sometimes, your father had to keep watch all night for rats in Ken's and Craig's room. He sat with an axe in his hand on a kitchen chair just outside their door. The rats liked to eat the paste that stuck the wallpaper to the wall."

We passed house after house that I could not remember living in, and a few that I could. "We've lived in a lot of houses, haven't we?" Jennie said, sighing, exhaling smoke.

"Why do we move so much?"

"If you do anything often enough, it grows on you."

"That's not why."

"No. We always thought the next house would be nicer. Every house looked nicer than the one that we were in. Don't all these houses look nicer than the one we're in now?"

I nodded. "Lucy says we move around like gypsies."

"Does she? Lucy has only lived in two houses in her life. What else does she say?"

"She says that, once you move often enough, you can't stop. You don't even know why you're moving anymore."

We came to a house with its lights on and someone sitting, bundled in a blanket, on the porch. An old man. He called, "Are you up late or up early, Jennie?"

"We're shopping for another house," Jennie said, and he laughed.

"How's your little boy?" he said. "Still sick?"

It was as if he thought I couldn't hear him.

"Not bad, tonight."

"It's a nice night," he said. "Spring and it's barely February. We'll pay for this in March."

"Probably."

We continued on. *Still sick*? It was one of the constants of life in the Goulds, that Jennie's boy would still be sick.

"Lucy is going to ask Luke Joyce to pray for me."

"A tapeworm hasn't got a chance against Luke Joyce. You didn't tell her we needed money for medicine, did you?"

"No."

"Make sure you don't."

"I *won't*."

"All right, all right. I haven't mentioned it to her, either. I'm waiting for the right time."

"When Ned is not there?"

"Something like that."

I asked her why Ned so rarely spoke. Jennie said Ned was a multiple-choice question with an endless number of answers. You might pick one you thought was right, but how could you be sure there wasn't a better one further down the page?

We walked on in silence for a while, heading back toward the house on the opposite side of the pond, where there was no room for houses between the road and the water.

"Too bad we couldn't just keep on walking," she said. "Walking and walking all the way to Petty Harbour. All the way to the ocean. We could watch the sun come up."

"That's far."

"Not really. If we *crossed* the ocean, that would be far."

We approached a convenience store with a light on inside that looked as if it would soon open for the day. It was owned and run by a woman named Mary Aggie, who, with her husband, Mike, made spruce beer they sold in the store for less than the cost of brewery beer. Jennie said she had yet to meet anyone who knew the trick of drinking it without coming away with a mouthful of spruce needles, but it sold very well.

Mary Aggie must have heard us, for the door opened and she came out on the small concrete steps, dressed in a cardigan and smoking a ragged, hand-rolled cigarette.

"Morning, Jennie," she said. "How's young Wayne?"

Jennie looked at me as if to say, "Well, tell her how you are."

"I'm fine," I said. When Mary Aggie smiled at me, I realized her question had been addressed to me.

"I was glad when I heard that you came back from St. John's," she said to Jennie. "I like it when your youngsters wait for the school bus in the store. Wayne was always the quiet one, unless you count his cough. But you're not coughing now, are you?"

I shook my head. "I walked all the way around the pond."

She smiled again. I'd forgotten how nice she was, how generous, allowing the children to wait in the warmth of her store in the winter even if they didn't buy anything. She sometimes even put out treats for us on the counter. My mouth watered as I remembered the sight of a tray of marshmallow squares, the marshmallow atop thick blocks of shortbread and sprinkled with coconut, the squares lying on a sheet of creased waxed paper—even the waxed paper looked inviting. Always, though, the marshmallow tasted so sickly sweet I couldn't swallow it and couldn't stand to look at the other children, Ken and Craig among them, as they devoured as many squares as they could cram into their mouths.

"Nice to see you again, Wayne," Mary Aggie called, as we pushed on up the road. "You, too, Jennie."

We waved goodbye and went home, arriving before anyone was out of bed.

While I was waiting for the others to get up and Jennie was making breakfast in the kitchen, I lay, half-reclined, on the bedmobile and read a book. I chose one that our walk around the pond had made me think of, *The Grapes of Wrath*.

I often read short stories and novels sooner than I was supposed to, even though I didn't really understand them. I was especially fond of literary novels that could be read as adventure stories. My favourites were those that involved odysseys that took their heroes far from home, like *Huckleberry Finn* or *Gulliver's Travels*.

Though I liked *The Grapes of Wrath*, I couldn't take seriously the supposed privations the Joads endured on their Dust Bowl road trip in quest of the lush paradise of California. Not only were they required to eat all my favourite foods, but they were able to keep them down—fried potatoes, fried ground beef, fried back bacon, fried eggs, fried beans, fried dough. Also, they got to spend their days and nights pursuing all the pastimes I would have pursued had I been able—sleeping out under the stars on clear, warm summer nights, sitting round campfires while singing songs, fishing in creeks for catfish, forever travelling by wagon to places they had never been, free of school work, never having to go to confession and try to remember if the sins I made up for Father McGettigan were different from the ones I had made up before—not that it mattered most of the time, because the second I stepped inside that musty little box, I began to cough.

In what sense Steinbeck intended the Joads to be pitiable, I had no idea. I wanted them to keep on doing what they were doing forever and never reach California, which sounded as nebulous, as dull and featureless as heaven. I wanted to trade the Johnston miseries for those of the Joads, with whom, I fancied, we did share a kinship in that we were both forever on the move, forever trading one place for another in an odyssey that would never end.

Over breakfast, Jennie told Dad that she and I had just come back from a walk and that I had told her that Lucy was going to ask Luke Joyce to pray for me.

"Well then," Dad said, "all our problems are solved."

"It can't hurt," Jennie said.

Dad said that the fact that something couldn't hurt didn't mean that it could help. There were an infinite number of other things that couldn't hurt—why didn't she try curing Wayne with those? What difference would it have made if Luke Joyce was the fifth son of an eighth daughter? Why did his being the seventh son of a seventh son give him special powers? Had Luke Joyce ever cured anyone of anything, or was it just that some of the ailments he prayed over simply went away on their own after a while and he got the credit for it—always the credit and never the blame, just as it was with God. It made people who lived where there was no doctor feel like they were being taken care of by a man who in all likelihood couldn't read or write. Dad threw up his hands. He said he couldn't find the words for what he thought of such backwardness or the many ways that people suffered from it. If Lucy asked Luke Joyce to pray for Wayne one more time—

Jennie said what would he do, stop going to the Crystal so she wouldn't have to ask her mother for money to pay the light bill anymore?

As they bickered/bantered, Craig said to me, "You went out walking with Jennie and your bamboo stick, and now you get to do nothing all day but hang around with Lucy, your other mommy. She's like you, afraid to go outdoors."

"I go outdoors."

"Only when someone is holding your hand. Jennie's Boy. Mommy's Boy. Lucy's Boy."

Jennie told Craig to stop picking at me. "Wayne did all his school work in one hour and that is why he has time to go for walks."

But Jennie regarded me guiltily as if, throughout her pregnancy, her body had failed mine and would forever be unable to make up for it. Craig said that he didn't bother with his school work at all, so he had more time for everything than I did. If I waited for being good at school to get me a girlfriend, the closest I would ever come to having one was Jennie, unless I got lucky with Lucy.

Jennie said that was no way to talk about your mother and grandmother.

Craig had once come out of the bunk room late at night when I was reading, and asked me to help him with math, which he would have figured out himself except it was so boring it made him fall asleep. I tried to help him, but he couldn't get it, not even the parts that seemed obvious to me, so he said it was no wonder I was good at it, because it wasn't as if it was something that would ever be of any use to anyone.

The pleasantness of the walk around the pond with Jennie and talking to Mary Aggie was spoiled. I remembered Jennie saying she wished we could have just gone on walking to the ocean to watch the sun come up, and I wished we had.

sixteen

By the time I got to Lucy's, I was in a foul mood that Lucy picked up on right away. I wanted to get back at *someone* for *something*, so I told her that Jennie would soon be asking her for money to pay for the medicine that no one but the doctors thought I needed. Jennie had warned me not to tell her, I said, so I asked her not to tell Jennie that I had.

"I won't," she said.

"Craig is always getting on my nerves."

Lucy said she had never seen such a crowd as us for getting on each other's nerves. Our nerves got on our nerves. She said the best thing to do when someone got on your nerves was to ignore them. The entire world got on Ned's nerves, so he ignored it. That was why he was never in a bad mood or any kind of mood, as far as she could tell.

"Craig said that I'm afraid to go outdoors by myself."

She said that if that was the best he could do by way of getting on my nerves, he'd never make a living at it.

After I had my chocolate Quik and submitted to my bath by water jug, I stayed in the front room, brooding over what Craig had said to me at breakfast, while she and Ned had lunch.

When we were through at the Shrine, I knelt on the chesterfield, looking out the window at the house across the road. Jennie would rather be alone than have me underfoot all day, so she pawned me off on Lucy. I felt that I should *do* something but I couldn't think of what until it occurred to me that I should prove to Craig that I could go outdoors by myself.

I knew that, even if they had no money, my brothers hung round together after school at a confectionery called Lee's, at the corner of Petty Harbour Road and the Goulds Road. They often *did* have money because Dad always left his pants on the bedroom floor after he had been to the Crystal, and Craig, if Jennie wasn't around, stole his change, figuring that Dad would never remember how much he had in his pockets.

I told Lucy that I was going to walk up Petty Harbour Road to meet them. She wondered if she should call Jennie and tell her of my plan. If she did, I said, Jennie would come with me, and I wanted to go on my own. It was just a ten-minute walk. It wasn't very cold outside. I would meet my brothers at Lee's and come home with them.

"What if Jennie sees you and comes running after you?" she said. I hadn't thought of that.

I told her I would go out the back way and cut across the meadow until I reached the road. Jennie's view of the meadow was blocked by a stand of pine trees.

Lucy pursed her lips dubiously. "You'll be all right?"

I rolled my eyes.

I got into my outdoor clothes, put on my boots and took my bamboo cane from the porch. I all but ran from the house, crossed the yard, ducked beneath the fence and made my way along the treeline to the road, by which time I was out of breath and coughing.

As I walked up Petty Harbour Road, I encountered boys who were headed home from the Protestant school just west of Kilbride. They didn't really know me, but they knew *of* me. Jennie's boy. Some of them waved to me and laughed and asked me if I was going fishing, but most of them ignored me.

When I reached the parking lot of Lee's, I was coughing so hard I doubled over and thought I might be sick.

The feeling passed but the cough persisted. My brothers weren't there yet, just a group of four boys, foster children, identifiable to me as such because they were smartly dressed, had new haircuts and new school supplies. They were each making a new beginning, staying with the Fleming family, who, since they were paid a stipend per boy, always took in more than they could manage. There was a great deal of turnover among the Fleming foster boys. Few of them lasted at St. Kevin's for more than a few months, though almost every one of them began well. They got good grades and were popular among the girls, who thought them exotic for being from town and, in many cases, for having done something that warranted a stay in a juvenile detention centre. Most of them were eventually caught stealing, or cheating, or they skipped school, and were sent back to where they came from.

One of the four caught my eye and waved. He was much taller than me, his blonde hair slicked with cream. I waved back, and he and the other three strolled over to where I stood. When I was still in school, I had always been intrigued by the Fleming foster boys. I had a notion that because, like the Johnstons, they were forever moving from house to house, their lives were an endless cycle of hope-reviving start-overs that were fated, through no fault of theirs, to go wrong.

The one who had waved asked if he could see my bamboo cane. I handed it to him and he assumed what I took to be some sort of martial arts stance, spinning the bamboo around, slashing at the air with it, holding it like a spear. He stopped and, smiling, looked down at me.

"Why do you carry this around?" he said. "Looks kind of funny."

"I use it to keep from falling," I said. "I can't use my left arm."

"Can't use it?"

"No. It's kind of paralyzed. A doctor gave me a needle the wrong way."

He raised his eyebrows. "Jesus," he said.

He was about to say something else when, from out of nowhere, Craig appeared and stepped between us. The foster boy was a couple of inches taller than him but slightly built.

"Give him back his friggin' cane," Craig said.

"Or what?" the foster boy said.

"Come on, Tommy," one of the other foster boys said. "Let's just get out of here."

"He wasn't doing anything, Craig," I said.

"Give him back his friggin' *cane*, ya friggin' greaser," Craig said.

"Or *what*?" Tommy said, laughing now.

Craig pushed him hard with both hands. Tommy fell backward, landing on his backside on the frozen, ice-glazed gravel, dropping the cane when he tried to soften his landing with the palms of his hands. When he held them up to look at them, they were scraped and bleeding.

"My pants are torn," Tommy said, his tone that of someone whose most precious possession had been ruined.

As I knelt to recover my cane, I was astonished to see Tommy's chin wobble as if he was about to cry.

A foster boy who was likely older than Tommy, with thick black eyebrows that all but joined in the middle, helped him to his feet, then stepped toward Craig. "Why don't you try pushing me?" he said.

Without a word, Craig slid out of his duffle coat and school blazer and handed them to Ken, who had appeared just behind Craig, Brian at his side.

"Come on, Craig," Ken said. "Let's just go home."

But Craig also removed his tie, handed it to Ken, and rolled up the sleeves of his white shirt. Eyebrows followed suit, handing his outer clothes and tie to Tommy. A large crowd of boys and girls quickly gathered round.

I thought that Craig and Eyebrows would push each other, or wrestle, try to throw each other to the ground—that was the only kind of fight I'd ever seen. Instead, they squared off like boxers, their fists in front of their faces, Craig seeming as accustomed to the stance as Eyebrows did.

Craig threw a jab that caught Eyebrows on the forehead but didn't seem to faze him. The crowd roared its approval, many of them shouting encouragement to Craig. Eyebrows, whose name even his fellow foster boys seemed not to know, threw a punch that hit Craig squarely on the nose, which began to bleed. Craig wiped away the water that came to his eyes.

"It's not too late to quit," Eyebrows said, just as Craig threw a right that landed squarely on his chin and knocked him onto his backside. A loud cheer went up.

They kept at it, taking turns knocking each other down, never blocking or ducking a punch.

I could see everyone's breath, but Craig and the other boy were breathing so hard they made a lot more mist. They sounded like panting dogs. Their faces bore blank looks of concentration. The gravel, being frozen, was hard to keep your balance on and didn't give at all when they fell. It tore through their clothes, through the knees of their slacks, through the elbows of their shirts and the skin on the palms of their hands. It hurt them more than they hurt each other with their fists. It drew more blood. I saw blood through the holes in their clothes, their grey school slacks stained dark with it, their shirts almost as red as they were white.

As Eyebrows scrambled to his feet after being knocked down for the umpteenth time, the fight was broken up in the strangest way. Two older boys who had just got off the Brother Rice and Holy Heart bus from town, wearing their maroon blazers, forced their way through the crowd and hoisted Craig by the underarms until he was clear of the ground and carried him in mid-air toward Petty Harbour Road, Craig protesting, fighting to get free of them and looking back over his shoulder at Eyebrows.

As the crowd dispersed, Ken, Brian and I ran after the boys who were carrying Craig away. Once they had put some distance between them and Lee's, they set him down, one patting him on the back.

"Beat you up, did he, Craig?" he said, looking at Craig's still-bleeding nose.

"Yeah, *right*," Craig said. "I knocked him on his arse about ten times."

Ken, Brian and I walked behind them, Ken red-faced, Brian crying and looking terrified. It must have been his first fight, too. My heart was pounding, but I wasn't coughing. I was flummoxed by all that had happened since Tommy borrowed my bamboo cane and the older boys broke up the fight by removing Craig from it the way they had. The two boys, chattering and grinning, moved on ahead of us. Soon after, we reached our driveway.

Craig said Jennie would be mad at him because she would have to buy him a whole new set of school clothes because she would never send him to school with clothes that were patched up. She'd be even madder if she knew that he'd been in a fight, so we were to say that he fell while he was running down a hill.

Ken said she would want to know which hill. She would want to know everything. And it didn't matter anyway because, by tomorrow, everyone would know that Craig had fought with Eyebrows.

"Just tell Mom I fell down," Craig said, taking his clothes from Ken and putting them back on. "No one say a word about the fight. Mom will pretend to believe me so that Dad won't get pissed off."

Craig got to the bunk room before Jennie could see him. I found him standing side on to the window, staring out, dabbing his nose with the back of his hand. He wore an expression of profound embitterment as if, out there in the backyard, lay the evidence that the universe was and always would be stacked against him.

"I didn't know you were so good at fighting," I said.

"You don't know anything," he said. "Why did you let him take your cane? You could have hit him with it. He's as big a sook as you are."

"He didn't take it. He asked if he could see it, and I gave it to him."

"What did you think he was going to do with your stupid stick, give it back to you? In two or three pieces maybe. You would have stood there doing nothing. You never *do* anything. You don't know how to do anything. Whatever it is, someone has to do it for you. You're afraid to try. You're afraid of everything. Gutless. You could have stood up for yourself. You could have told him to frig off. He picked on you because he knew you wouldn't fight back. He can't fight. His friend had to do his fighting for him, just like I had to do yours for you. You're two years older than Brian and he's better at everything than you are. We're all sick of sticking up for you. You spoil *every*thing.

You and that stick and your stupid broken teeth. You don't even know what you *look* like. You should see yourself. Everyone makes fun of you at school. They laugh at *us* because we're your brothers. *How's Jennie's boy? Is he dead yet?"*

"They don't say that."

"Well, maybe they don't say *that*. They know what would happen if they did. They don't say that. I made that up. But they say lots of other things."

"Like what?"

"Never mind. No one ever hit you in the face. You don't know what it's like. You never hit anyone in the face. You don't know what *that's* like. You don't even go to school anymore. Other people look out for you, but you don't look out for anyone, not even Brian. I have to look out for him, too, and even for Ken because he can't fight. He's not afraid to, but he's no good at it. So I look out for everyone, but no one, not even Dad, looks out for me.

"I don't give a frig. That's okay. I don't care. You're sick. It's not your fault. Those two big guys from Brother Rice thought they were looking out for me. They're not so bad. But they'll tell everyone that the guy from Fleming's beat me up. Everyone will think I lost because they picked me up and carried me down Petty Harbour Road. He beat up Craig Johnston. You just watch. That's what everyone will say. I don't care. That foster boy will get kicked out of Fleming's. Maybe Tommy, too. So I don't care. I'll still be at St. Kevin's. Maybe. Unless we move to town again.

"I might have a girlfriend soon. You won't. Not for a long time. Maybe never. Not never, but you'll have to grow up first, so maybe never. Girls your size are six years old. You're not so bad, but you could be better if you tried. Not a lot better, but a bit better. You like books, so how much better can you get? Girls like guys who don't like books. Some girl who likes books might pick you because there's no one left."

Perhaps because I looked especially desolate, he did what he always did. He told me he'd been kidding and that I wasn't as bad as he said I was. He hugged me so hard it hurt and tousled my hair. He welled up but he didn't cry. I did.

"You're not so bad," he said. "You might get a *bit* better, right?"

I nodded, tears streaming down my face. "I will," I said. "I promise."

"You haven't got much to work with, that's the problem. Maybe if you just shoot for a *bit* better, that would be something."

I said I would shoot for a bit better. I said I wished I wasn't such a dork. I wished I didn't cough so much. I wished I didn't have to use the stupid bedmobile. Maybe if I wasn't up all night, I wouldn't be so tired and so sick, and I would keep more food down. I told him I was sorry he had to do my fighting for me. I went on and on. He soon went back to looking out the window and dabbing at his bloody nose, but he nodded each time I apologized for one of the many things he had ever said was wrong with me.

I thought about it a lot. Why hadn't I seen why Tommy wanted my stupid stick? How was it that I could never tell what people were *really* like, what they were *really* thinking? Why was it clear to Craig but not to me?

seventeen

The next day, at Lucy's, as we were kneeling at the Shrine, I told her some of the things Craig had said.

"Well," she said, "he was just in a fight and still wiping the blood off his face. He isn't often in a good mood, but bleeding has never been known to bring one on.

"You got off to a good start after you were born, you know, even after all the trouble your mother had when she carried you. You were only three pounds, but you put on weight for a while. You were big when you were six months old, but you ran out of gas pretty fast. At first, I thought you might grow up to be bigger than your older brothers. You went through more jars of baby food than the two of them put together. All the things you turn up your nose at now you loved back then— spinach, broccoli, beets, prunes. As long as it was baby food. Your face was always a mess. But you never really made the turn to solid food. I suppose you could have stuck with baby food, but how would that look when you grew up?

"You were always laughing. You loved being played with. You slept through the night without a sound. You were walking by eleven months. Then something in your nature changed. You started to backslide. You went completely off the rails. Wouldn't eat. Wouldn't sleep. You stopped walking and went back to crawling. Whoever heard of that? You soured on everything and everything soured on you.

"I never saw such crookedness in a child. Bawling all the time. More things turned on you than turned on the Egyptians. The Plagues of Wayne, Jennie called it. You caught the worst case of whatever was going around. Measles, chicken pox, hives, scarlet fever, pink eye, bronchitis. You had pneumonia more than once. 'I might as well try to toilet train a rabbit,' Jennie said. No child ever drove its parents closer to going cracked than you did."

She glanced at me then and said, "It wasn't your fault. No one gets sick just to make trouble. I still pray to the patron saint of sick children for you. Saint Hugh, he's called. Mind you, he's also the patron saint of swans, whatever sense that makes. If there was a patron saint of cranky babies, he would have heard from Jennie more than once by now."

I wondered if I should ask her if Jennie had spoken to her about a loan to buy my medicine. I had begun to lose the hope I'd once had that, barring any worsening of my ailments, the matter of treating them might be deferred until it was forgotten. How serious a heart murmur could I have if all these days had passed without Jennie or Dad having said a word about it? The stomach man had been all but certain that I didn't have a tapeworm. The lung man was in the process of ruling out pulmonary fibrosis. My arm, Jennie had said, would recover on its own. Perhaps my parents had decided that near certainty about all the rest was good enough. But I wasn't so sure.

There were times when I couldn't help dwelling on what murmur surgery would be like. I had seen many pictures of the Sacred Heart—Jesus wearing robes but with his lurid red heart showing through them, Jesus with his heart outheld in one hand, looking like he had just knocked on someone's door and was offering the heart for sale.

Open-hearted people were kind and generous, but open-heart surgery involved cutting into your heart, which you needed more than anything except your brain. The Sacred Heart was sometimes wound with barbed wire. I imagined a tapeworm coiled around my heart.

The idea that doctors considered it possible for someone to have a tapeworm inside them made me wonder what other things might be capable of getting in. The thought of a tape-worm having set up house inside *me*, the thing forever coiled like a snake, waiting for food to come its way, was doing nothing to increase what little appetite I had.

What if the tapeworm decided someday that it was time to move on? The Johnstons were always doing that. How would it get out and how would I explain it to whoever happened to be around when it made its bid for freedom through one of my nostrils or my mouth?

I looked at the photograph of Ned and Leonard on that sunny day in the hayfield. Lucy had once told me that tuberculosis was the only thing Leonard had ever come down with. He hadn't been sickly by nature, like me. I felt certain that no one had ever ripped into him as Craig had ripped into me. Now he was the centre of Lucy's house—the sad centre, but the centre of it nonetheless.

"Let's say our prayer," Lucy said as she lit the votive candle. "I'll say one for you and you say one for me, all right?"

I nodded, feeling guilty for having so often only pretended to pray with her.

Lucy's eyes were shut so tight her whole face was a grimace—such was the effort, it seemed to me, that she thought was needed to bring about the slightest improvement in me. But then I saw that she was grimacing with pain.

"Go out to the porch and get that bamboo cane of yours," she said, through clenched teeth.

I got up and hurried out of the room and down the hall to the kitchen just in time to see Murchie dart back beneath the daybed. I grabbed my cane from where it leaned against the porch wall and ran back to the Shrine to find Lucy on her knees, supporting herself with both hands on the table that bore Mary and the Baby Jesus, her rosary cast aside on the bed.

"Give me the cane," she said, grabbing it from me with her right hand before I could extend it to her. "You support me on the other side."

"I only have one good arm," I said. "I'll tip over."

"I forgot," she said, and sighed. "Then I'll lean on the bed, but I'm afraid the mattress might sink too much."

I had never felt more useless in my life. I put my good hand under her arm. "I can lift you a bit."

"All right." Still grimacing with pain, she put her free hand on the mattress and planted the cane on the floor. With a great grunt of exertion, she rose up slowly with little help from me and managed to roll sideways onto the bed, the cane beside her, her chest and stomach heaving, her eyes fixed on the ceiling as if in astonishment that her body could hurt her so much.

I felt the urge to cry and cough but managed to do neither. "What's wrong?"

"My condition is acting up," she said.

"I'll get Dot Chafe." I was relieved to have thought of something I was actually able to do.

"Dot's at work," she said as her breathing became somewhat less laboured.

"Then I'll get Jennie or Ned," I said.

"No, you *won't* or you'll never see another glass of chocolate Quik. Just lie down on the bed beside me and we'll have a nap. Or I will, and you can do whatever you do when other people are asleep. I'm all right, don't worry. I just need to rest."

So I lay down beside her. There was just room on the bed for the two of us. I immediately began what promised to be a prolonged bout of coughing.

"Sit up and lean against the wall," she said. "Hold my hand. I might need to squeeze yours now and then. I can rest without going to sleep. It wouldn't be the first time. We'll talk about what we were talking about before."

Me, in other words. I felt foolish, selfish. But I did what she said.

I poured it all out, the persecution of Dad at the party by her three sons, the seemingly universal assumption that I wouldn't live to see puberty, the fact that I played a part in no one's vision of the future and that a baby to take my place was on the way—five years since Brian was born, seven years since I was born. The shape of the family had seemed to be set in stone, but soon another baby would arrive.

Lucy asked me if I knew how a woman came to be with child. With Child. I had only ever heard that said of the Blessed Virgin. As if she had read my mind, she said that Jennie, blessed though she was in many ways, was not a virgin.

Just to see what she would say, I asked her what a virgin was. She said a woman who had never known a man. I told her I knew what she meant by "known." She looked relieved. I told her that a woman got to know a man in a bedroom on Sunday afternoons when the door was closed and the radio was playing really loud. She smiled and said that was exactly right.

She said it was partly her fault that her boys were the way they were. They could make the most chaste of monks feel like an idiot for remaining celibate. They had inherited her way of speaking but not her sense of when it was right to speak that way, though she admitted that she sometimes crossed the line because, when you spent as much time alone as she did, you had to keep yourself entertained.

But she said that Dad was partly to blame for what happened at the party because he would tempt the most tolerant of all the saints into mocking him. The Bible was just fairy tales? Maybe no one made the world? Dad couldn't go around saying things like that and expect to be ignored by men who, on top of believing every word of the Bible, didn't exactly get as much fulfillment from climbing out of bed at four in the morning to milk the cows as he did from getting up at eight to catch a bus or drive a car to work.

When she at last fell asleep, I lay inclined against the wall and listened to her breathing, glad that her condition was no longer acting up. What a wondrous thing untroubled sleep seemed to be. She, at her age, could manage it, but I could not.

After about an hour, she opened her eyes.

"I feel a bit better," she said. "You get up first."

I did, and she took hold of my cane, planted it on the floor and managed to reach a sitting position, her legs hanging over the bed.

"I can get Dad to make you a cane like that," I said.

With some effort, she stood up, then held the cane out to me.

"That's fine," she said. "I might borrow it again, though."

After I got home, I was about to tell Jennie that Lucy's condition had acted up when the phone rang. It was Dot Chafe calling to say that Lucy was sick.

Lucy had called her just after I left. Dot had called Dr. McIntyre, who made a quick house call. After examining Lucy, he recommended that she go to the hospital. Lucy refused to go. Then, when the doctor was gone, she called Dot again to say that she was feeling much worse. Dot said she thought that Jennie better get over there.

Jennie held a kitchen meeting to tell us that she would be staying at Ned and Lucy's—she wasn't sure for how long—and that Dad would need to take some vacation days so that he could look after us.

"I'll be just across the road," she said, fighting back tears. Soon after, she left for Lucy's with the battered suitcase Dad took with him when he toured the fish plants on the South Coast.

Dad turned on the TV and the five of us watched it in silence. Every so often, I went into my parents' room and looked out the window at Lucy's house, which was dark but for a flicker of blue light at the front, which meant that Ned, too, was watching TV.

I spent the night in the living room, obsessively monitoring the house across the way, fretting that an ambulance would come down the dark road, siren wailing. Pancreatitis—it sounded as gravely exotic as the words for all the things that were wrong with me. No wonder Lucy preferred to say it was her condition that was acting up.

All night, a room on the side of the house remained dimly lit. Jennie tending to Lucy? Merely talking to her or sleeping in a chair beside her bed. One or the other of them, alone, unable to sleep, Jennie perhaps sneaking a cigarette and listening for sounds in the house in which she had spent her childhood.

eighteen

On Saturday, after Dad made us a lunch of Vienna sausage sandwiches, he said, "Let's go for a drive up the Shore, boys."

"Yeah," Craig said. We all thought it was a good idea. The proximity of the house in which Lucy lay ill with some disease we knew nothing about, tended by our mother, had us in a funk of boredom and anxiety.

Up the Shore meant we were going to Ferryland. We hadn't been there in several years, though it had been our custom to go once a month in the summer, when the road was at its best, a routine we had fallen out of during a long stretch when we didn't have a car. We used to visit his parents' house and those of many aunts and uncles, explore the beach with our first cousins and walk out to the lighthouse. Craig had mastered the art of spearing bottom-dwelling sand dabs, a kind of flounder, from the wharf, which I usually stayed clear of because, whenever I looked down into the water and saw the seemingly far-distant ocean floor, I got dizzy and almost fell in.

After Dad phoned Jennie to tell her where we were going, we piled in the car, Dad and Ken in the front, the rest of us in the back, with me in the middle.

"Have to gas up," Dad said, turning right at the intersection of Petty Harbour and the Goulds Roads.

We didn't reach the gas station. After about a mile and a half, Dad turned into the huge parking lot of the Crystal Palace, which was about one-quarter full of the cars of weekend patrons.

"We better not be stopping here," Craig said.

"We better not," I said.

Dad said nothing, just parked near the entrance to the sprawling white building, which at one time had been a barn. There was a marquee on the front whose lights, even at one in the afternoon, were flashing, spelling out in large letters, "The Crystal Palace: Dancing and Entertainment," the words surrounded by drawings of music notes and cocktail glasses and tuxedo-clad men dancing with curvaceous women in tight dresses.

"What are we stopping here for, Dad? You said you were taking us up the Shore." Craig struck the back of Dad's seat with the palm of his hand.

"I'll just be a minute," Dad muttered. "I'm just going in to say a quick hello to someone."

"Come *on*, Dad," Craig said, "you *told* us."

"I'll be right out," Dad said.

"You're not supposed to spend the rent," Craig said.

"And the money for Wayne's medicine," Brian piped up as Dad, puffing on a cigarette, pushed his door open, quickly got out and shut it behind him.

"We'll tell Jennie," Craig shouted as Dad hurried across the gravel lot to the steps of the Crystal, climbed them two at a time and went inside.

Craig told Ken to honk the horn, but Ken merely looked out the front passenger window and fingered the white tape at the corner of his glasses. Craig started to climb over the seat, but Ken pushed him back. Craig told him to start honking the horn and keep honking it.

"Then *every*one will come out," Ken said. "Everyone except him."

"I bet there are no kids in any of the other cars," Craig said, looking around us.

Brian said it was a good thing that we were wearing our winter coats, because it wasn't all that warm in the car.

"By the time he comes out, it will be dark and freezing," Craig said.

"It won't be dark," Ken said.

"Push the cigarette lighter in, Ken," Craig said. "Push it in and leave it in until it gets hot and pops out."

"What for?" Ken said. "The lighter won't make it any warmer."

"It'll run down the battery," Craig said. "We could turn on the lights, too."

"That wouldn't make Dad come out any sooner," Ken said.

"But we could get *back* at him," Craig said. He banged the back of the seat again as if Dad was still sitting behind the wheel.

"Everyone going in and coming out will see us sitting in the car like a bunch of *babies*," Craig said. "Scrunch down. They'll know it's his car. They'll know he left us in it by ourselves."

Craig didn't want to be seen sitting in the car, abandoned by the father who had fooled him into thinking we were going up the Shore, played on him the kind of trick that only a sook like me would fall for. But none of us scrunched down.

"Don't say anything when he comes out. Not a word."

Ken said that was a good idea because giving him the silent treatment when he was too drunk to notice would really show him who was boss.

There were tears of spite in Craig's eyes. "Friggin' Dad," he said.

"Maybe he'll come out soon and *then* we'll go up the Shore," I said, even though I knew there was no chance it would happen. I hoped it would provoke Craig into picking on me, which I thought would make him feel better.

"Don't be so friggin' *stoopid*," Craig said. He swore he wasn't sitting all afternoon in the back seat with Brian and me. This time when he climbed over the seat and sat behind the wheel, Ken didn't try to stop him. "I'm not sittin' here all day," Craig said. "I'm gettin' out and goin' home. We all should. He'd get a good fright if he came out and the car was empty."

"If you walk home, everyone in the Goulds will see you," Ken said. "Everyone knows Jennie is looking after Lucy. Someone will tell her they saw you. They'll call her on the phone. Then Jennie will know that something's wrong, and she'll have to try to get someone else to look after Lucy because she'll have to look after you and find someone to go to the Crystal to take us home. Besides, it's too far for Wayne to walk."

"His arm is paralyzed, not his legs."

"Stay in the car," Ken said.

"Friggin' Dad." Craig couldn't stop. "I should have known he wouldn't drive up the Shore in this old heap of junk." He said he should have known Dad wasn't turning over a new leaf just because Lucy was sick and Jennie needed him to pitch in. Wayne had been sick since he was born, but that hadn't made Dad turn over any leaves. He'd never turned over a leaf in his life, and that was why we lived like gypsies. Jennie should have known he'd get up to something. But when she ripped into him, she always took it back. We all did. Ripping in was just a waste of time if you took it back. It didn't teach anybody any lessons. Dad had Jennie wrapped around his finger. No one had Craig wrapped around their finger, but you weren't supposed to leave boys in cars in parking lots when their grandmother had whatever the frig it was Lucy had. He hadn't seen it coming, but who could imagine their father doing that?

"We'll just stay put," Ken said. "He might not be all that long."

"As long as it takes to spend the rent," Craig said. We'd be in a tent soon. Half the people in the Goulds didn't even have jobs, but they had cars and houses. They weren't on the move like nomads all the time.

"When's he coming out?" Brian said. "I'm getting cold."

"He won't be out until it's dark," Craig said.

"Maybe he doesn't have much money," Ken said.

Craig said he always got his hands on it no matter where

Jennie hid it. At that point, Craig wiped his nose with the back of his hand as tears began to stream down his distorted face. Brian began to cry, too.

"Now you got *him* started," Ken said.

"We could let the air out of the tires," Craig said. "He'll have four flats when he comes out. He probably wouldn't even notice until we were down to the wheel rims."

"That would just be *us* spending the rent," Ken said. "He'd have to get a tow truck."

Two elderly men walked past the car but seemed not to notice us. They climbed the steps and went inside.

"We could just get out and sit on the car or walk around if it's not too cold," I said. "That's what I do when he comes here after we go fishing."

"This is your fault," Craig said. "You let him get away with it. You should have ripped into him. You never rip into anyone. I'm not sitting on the car like some little dork waiting for his daddy. Do people come out and pat you on the head?"

Ken told him to knock it off.

"Jennie knows he comes here after we go fishing," I said. "But he might not take me at all if she put her foot down."

Craig said it didn't matter anymore because who could fish with one arm paralyzed by a booster shot? Most of me didn't work anymore, not even my brain. Who would be dumb enough to let a giant worm crawl down their throat?

Ken laughed, so I did, too. Then I started to cough and couldn't stop. Craig said the worm must have woken up. Brian patted me on the back. The coughing got worse and I doubled over. My chest and back hurt.

"Friggin' Dad," Craig said.

"Let's all get out so Wayne can get some air," Ken said.

Craig opened the door and pulled me from the car by my arm. "Get sick if you have to," he said. "No one will see. There's no one around."

"Someone might come out," I said. I straightened up and the coughing got worse. Dots swarmed in front of my eyes, and Ken caught me beneath the arms as I began to fall. He and Craig sat me on the back bumper. I eventually stopped coughing, but my insides felt scorched. Pleurisy. Inflammation of the lining of the lungs. My insides were in flames.

"Maybe I should go in and tell Dad that you're sick," Ken said.

"I'll go," Craig said and ran up the steps and went inside before Ken could protest.

We waited for ten more minutes, but no one came out.

"We'll all go in," Ken said.

Brian said he'd never been in the Crystal. He sounded excited. I'd never been in there, either, and might have been excited, too, but I could barely breathe.

Ken helped me up the steps, then pulled open the green, leather-padded door.

I couldn't see a thing at first. I hadn't known that the Crystal, like most bars, was dimly lit. I all but gagged on the cigarette smoke and the smell of beer. There wasn't much noise, just the low hum of conversing voices, the occasional clatter of a dish. When my eyes adjusted to what little light there was, I saw a gleaming hardwood floor, an expanse of tables and empty chairs, long, narrow tables joined end to end, smaller round tables strewn with beer bottles and ash trays, with men and only men sitting at them, hunched over, one man passed out with his head on his arms.

All of the serving staff were women, dressed in green pinafores over white blouses. They paid no more attention to the three of us than they did to the passed-out man, weaving among the tables with trays bearing bottles of beer expertly balanced at head height on one hand.

Finally, a woman without a tray stopped in front of us and smiled. "Hi, boys," she said. Ken said hi back. "Who are you looking for?" she said, bending down, her hands on her knees.

"Art Johnston," Ken said.

The woman looked at me. "You're a long way from shipshape, my love."

"We have to get him home," Ken said.

"Yes, you do," she said. "I think your brother is down by the wall with your dad. You come with me. What did he do, leave you in the car?"

Ken nodded. She shook her head and frowned.

We followed her among the tables, at which men who paid us no mind were tipping back dark drinks from small glasses. Then I saw Dad sitting alone at a round table, his back to the rear wall as if he had situated himself so as to be able to survey the entire bar.

The men at the tables near his were laughing but also looking fed up.

Not until I was about to wave to Dad was I able to make out Craig, standing just to Dad's left, his hands gripping Dad's upper right arm, which Dad was keeping rigid at his side.

"There they are," the woman said. "I'll go get Frank."

She turned and headed toward the front at a brisk pace.

"Help me get him up, Ken," Craig said. Brian started to cry. I stared at Dad, who seemed to stare back. My cough returned.

Ken took hold of Dad's left arm. "Come on, Dad," he said. "Get up. Lucy is sick and Wayne is sick—"

"Wayne is right there," Dad said as if to contradict him. His voice was slurred.

"Thanks be to Jesus *you* boys showed up," a bearded man in a checkered shirt said from the next table over, adding that, in all the history of welcomes, none was ever more worn out than Dad's was. "When the wife sends a posse of youngsters out to get you, it's time to go home."

Another man looked with wary irony at me, wincing every time I coughed. "Which part of the car did you cram that youngster into, Art, the exhaust pipe?"

"He shouldn't be out of bed," Dad said.

"*You* should *never* be out of bed," the man replied.

As if he was attending to voices that no one else could hear, Dad cocked his head and smiled knowingly. "'A posse of youngsters,'" Dad said. "Good way to put it. Clever way. Forever chasing after me. Deputized to bring me home. Dead or alive."

"Dead will do," someone said.

"I've left better men than you in the dust," Dad said, then drank deeply from a glass of beer. The table in front of him bore at least a dozen bottles.

He was right, the man replied, and there were few with sufficient mental acumen to appreciate just how right he was, but even so, if Dad would allow him a token word in his defence, he might want to consider that others were entitled to an occasional break from domesticity and it was not unreasonable to expect that such a break—that fleeting interval during which a man who had earned it might relax—would not involve four boys storming into and shaming that man out of the Crystal like some pipsqueak temperance brigade.

"Frank will be here soon," a voice in the darkness said.

"Come on now, Art, not in front of your boys."

"In front of them. Behind them. As long as it's anywhere but here. Art Johnston and the Prohibition Boys. Hopefully not held over for a second week."

One man stood and looked about him at some others.

"Come on, Joe," he said, "let's help the boys out before that little one bursts a blood vessel."

Another man rose from his chair and looked at me. "Hang in there," he said. "Two of us will drive you all home."

Dad pulled his arms free of Ken and Craig. "I had dreams," he said.

"Is there not one priest in all the land who will hear this man's confession?" the bearded man said. "Or is there no one short of Christ himself who would be able to endure it?"

"*Dreams*," Dad said. "Have you never dreamed?"

The bearded man said that he had dreamed the night before that he went to the Crystal and Art Johnston wasn't there.

"There was a time when the smart money was on me," Dad said.

"Yes, and there was a time when the smart money was on Portugal."

Did people think he was happy to be paying a man so that his family could live in half a house? Dad asked the room. "Half a house. No upstairs. Blocked off. Windows boarded up. Paying rent for *that*?"

The bearded man said he bet that all the best furniture was up there and Dad shouldn't let a few boards and nails prevent him from getting at it.

Did they think, Dad said, that twenty years ago, this was the future he imagined for himself?

The bearded man asked if Dad thought that, on Friday, this was the Saturday afternoon that the present patrons of the Crystal had imagined for themselves, a game-of-cards-interrupting disquisition on the unfairness of not being able to choose your lot in life from a man who, it might well be, was about to spruce up the story of that life with the help of an overhead projector.

"It wasn't me that put me in the fix I'm in," Dad said. "The deck is stacked. Why *can't* I be the one who decides what my lot in life should be? I haven't got air of my own to breathe. Four youngsters hanging off of me and one more, one more at least, on the way. Not much room for dreams. One of the four more trouble than the other three combined. I might as well have seven or eight."

Had it occurred to Art Johnston, the bearded man asked, that to be told that having four children was unbearable was not what a man who had six at home wanted to hear a hundred times during the few hours a week he had away from them? Also, if Mr. Johnston didn't shut his gob, the bearded man would exact from him a greater toll in ten minutes than four of history's worst children could in twenty years.

"Jennie—"

"Oh, saints preserve us—Father, if it is possible, let this Cup be taken from me."

"Jennie was never one for dreams. No nonsense. Put your dreams aside. Face up to what you are. Make the best of a bad lot. Thank God for what you have. Remember your place, your rung on the ladder. Trying to be more than you were born to be will break your heart. Be happy with your little lot. A better world awaits. Fairy tales and superstition. A Crystal Palace in the sky."

If Jennie was his wife, the bearded man interjected, the only thing preventing her from being the patron saint of sad sack husbands was that she still drew breath.

Dad said that he had often been the butt of jokes told by lesser men, and the bearded man wondered if there was no one in the Crystal who was not only an exemplar of Christian kindness but also knew where a gun and a bullet might be found.

Dad said that suicide was a terrible thing.

"You're a bitter little man, aren't you?" the bearded man said.

"Not bitter, no. Nor little. Your wife will vouch for me."

"Yours has done much more for me than vouch. It's time you were told who the fathers of your children are."

At that, the bearded man overturned his table, sending glasses and ashtrays crashing to the floor. His two tablemates took hold of him but looked as if they wouldn't be able to restrain him for long. More red-faced, I imagined, than I had ever been, he struggled to get free, making a kind of swimming motion with his arms, clawing at the air with his fingers.

A couple of the other men got Dad to his feet, one of them saying it was remotely possible that the bearded man was on the verge of doing more than talk.

A man I took to be the long-ago-sent-for Frank came running to assist in getting the bearded man back into his chair.

Luckily, Dad was not so drunk that he needed assistance to walk, though the two men guided him toward the door, each with a hand under one of his elbows, as we followed.

"He leaves, captured by his posse of youngsters," the bearded man shouted. "I hope to God they don't forget the last one. More appealing things than that boy were banished for their ugliness from the sulphur pits of hell."

I heard the sound of more breaking glass behind me but dared not turn round to look. My cough had become a throat-shredding bark.

"Poor little fella," I heard someone say and suddenly felt so sorry for myself that, if not for the primary need to escape as fast as possible, I would have burst out bawling.

I avoided making eye contact with anyone. Dad's words kept running through my head. *One more trouble than the other three combined.* I knew I was more trouble than the other three combined, but I'd hated to hear him say it, especially in public.

It seemed to me that our march from the Crystal was a very long one indeed and that all the attention was centred on me, not only because of my appearance but also because I lagged behind the others, coughing so hard I was unable to keep up, terrified that I'd throw up and thereby raise this afternoon to an even loftier perch of infamy than it was already destined for.

Perhaps, in the wake of my father's monologue of self-pity and self-loathing, it was inevitable that I take stock of myself in like manner: needle-numbed runt, house-budget-draining nuisance, weakling who couldn't fight his own fights, guileless dork who would fall for any trick . . . I couldn't get out of the darkness of the Crystal and into the light of day fast enough.

The two men held tight to Dad's arms as they led him down the steps.

"He must have *planned* to get plastered," one of the men said. "He parked right by the steps. I never saw a man put beer away so fast." They helped him into the back seat of the Dart and plucked the keys from the pocket of his jacket.

One of them took Dad home in our Dodge and the other, without saying a word, drove the four of us in his car. As we pulled into the driveway, we saw the first man help Dad out of the car, walk with him to the back door and give him back his keys. The other man stayed in his car as we piled out. Craig almost caught up with Dad as he pushed the door open with his shoulder and stumbled inside.

By the time I made it to the hall, Dad had gone into his bedroom and closed the door.

"Friggin' Dad," Craig said. Tears were streaming freely down his face, though his voice was steady. "We should have walked home like I said. We could have gone down to the Lower Goulds and snuck back up behind the house. Jennie wouldn't have seen us. Now she'll probably be here any second."

"That would have been *way* farther than Wayne could walk," Ken said. "Especially through the woods."

Craig looked at me. I thought he was going to rip into me, but he hugged me instead. "It's not your fault," he said. "The three of us will get a going-over at school about this, and you'll get off scot-free, but it's not your fault."

nineteen

It seemed all but impossible that Jennie or Dot Chafe hadn't noticed the arrival of the two cars and the man getting out to escort Dad to the back of the house and the four of us climbing out of the other car and running after them.

I peered out the window. I saw Ned on the lower meadow, lugging two buckets of water toward the barn.

Lucy's front window blinds were closed, as were the curtains of the facing bedroom and those of the bedroom on the driveway side of the house. It looked like there might be lights on inside, though it was an hour from twilight.

Still, it would not have surprised me to see the front door open and Jennie come out and cross the road. But she didn't.

Ken, Craig and Brian went to their room and someone closed the door. I soon heard Ken and Craig talking in low tones, Craig's voice rising sometimes, though he didn't sound angry anymore. After a while, they stopped talking and one of them turned the radio on to a music station and turned up the volume.

I looked at my bed, which stood on its wheels against the wall beside my desk in the dining room. I couldn't stand the sight of it. The bedmobile. I pictured myself pushing it to the back door and sending it clattering down the steps.

I wondered how Lucy was doing and when I would get to tell her my version of what had happened at the Crystal, for I was certain she'd hear others.

After seeing Dad at the Crystal and hearing his every word undercut by the bearded man, I was also certain that none of my ailments would ever be attended to. There would be no drugs, no invasive procedures or surgeries, and I didn't care. I felt in the mood to *do* something. I didn't know what, other than that it should be something I had never done before.

The music in the bunk room grew louder, Ken and Craig taking advantage of Jennie's absence and Dad's transgressions. I crept to the door of Jennie and Dad's room, turned the knob and eased the door open an inch.

Dad was under the blankets, the steady rise and fall of which convinced me that he had passed out. I opened the door another inch and saw his slacks on the floor at the foot of the bed. I slipped into the room and tiptoed across the hardwood floor to the slacks. I crouched down, using my right hand for balance. I turned the slacks over so that the pockets were face up. Teetering on my toes, I fished in one pocket and my fingers closed on what felt like a quarter, then another, and a dime and a nickel. I fished in the other pocket but came up empty.

Sixty-five cents. I stood, crept back across the room and eased the door closed.

So I had done it, stolen from my dad like my brother Craig had been doing for years. But I could think of absolutely nothing to do with the sixty-five cents. Other boys would have gone to the store and bribed some grown-up to buy them cigarettes or beer. I had once taken a few drags of a cigarette and had had a coughing fit that lasted for hours. I had got hold of a bottle of spruce beer one summer from Lucy's fridge, having often seen the green bottle, covered in condensation, in the hands of men and older boys, who tipped it up and drank without stopping, then sighed, "Ahhhh," as if, in all of history, no thirst had ever been more exquisitely slaked. By way of small sips, I had managed half the bottle, then threw up. I was sick for a week and thereafter made nauseous by the very smell of spruce trees.

The more I looked at those coins, the more obliged I felt to commit some act of epic indulgence. What if I were to try to force myself to drink a six-pack of spruce beer *and* smoke a pack of cigarettes? I would either fail in the attempt and perish, or succeed with the same result. I thought of the amount of sweets I could buy—a feast of candy, homemade fudge, marshmallow squares, raisin squares and apple flips—but I knew I would never make my way through them. Sated was something I had never been and would never be, satedness a state that I would never achieve.

One more trouble than the other three combined. I have often been the butt of the jokes of lesser men.

Talk about the afternoon would get around. Four boys in the Crystal because their father left them in his car. The running commentary of the bearded man, the fight that had broken out as we were leaving, some other man picking up for Dad, picking up for me. *I hope to God they don't forget that last one.*

What a fool the bearded man had made of Dad, who had a reckoning coming, a ripping into from Jennie such as he had never had before. At least I had stolen from him, but he would never know unless I told him. But Jennie—

Not until then did it occur to me that, if Social Services was keeping tabs on us, we were sure to hear from them soon. Four young brothers in the Crystal, having gone in there to extricate their father? This was the playing out of just the sort of public spectacle that Jennie dreaded most. We were almost certain to have a visit from a welfare officer, and I, the very portrait of neglect, might be removed.

The loud music coming from the bunk room—my brothers were trying to drown out their dread of what would descend upon the house when Jennie found out and she and Dad went at each other in the kitchen. I looked again at the money in my hand. Sixty-five cents. More money by far than I had ever had in my life. I put it in the pocket of my pants.

I was about to go to the bunk room when the front door opened and Jennie, her eyes puffy from crying, hurried in. I thought she had come over to have it out with Dad until I saw, through the open door behind her, that Ned's yard was filled with cars and pickup trucks.

Craig stuck his head out of the bunk room, but Jennie didn't look at him. She put one hand on my shoulder and smoothed the front and back of my shirt over and over with the other.

"Lucy wants to see you," she said.

"What's goin' on, Jennie?" Craig called.

"Lucy is very sick, sweetheart," she said. "Is your father in bed?"

Craig paused, then said, "He's taking a nap."

Wiping her eyes with the heel of one hand, Jennie nodded blankly as if it made perfect sense for Dad to be napping, leaving the four of us unsupervised.

"Lucy wants to see Wayne," Jennie said, telling him more than that with her eyes and the tone of her voice. "I'll send someone over to stay here until I get back, all right?" Of course, she had guessed that Dad was in no shape to be woken up. Casting a furtive glance at me, Craig nodded and closed the door of the bunk room.

Lucy is very sick. How sick could she be? It was only a few days since I'd last seen her. "She asked to see you," Jennie said, smoothing a lock of my hair into place. *That* was how sick Lucy was.

"Do I have to get a bath and put on my good clothes?"

"You're fine as you are," Jennie said and managed a smile. "Just get your coat." I grabbed it from the chair where I'd thrown it. She put her hand on the small of my back and guided me toward the door. I wondered if she'd noticed the jingle of coins in my pocket—an unprecedented sound.

We went out and she closed the door behind us, then took me by my good hand and led me down the driveway and past the car. Across the road, vehicles were still arriving from both directions.

"Dot sent the word out," she said. "A lot of people haven't seen Lucy in a long time."

Two cars going in opposite directions stopped to let us cross the road, then took turns pulling into the farm. We wound our way among the vehicles until we reached the back door, which was open.

People were filing in one at a time, silent, solemn looking. I heard someone say, "Jennie's boy."

Jennie led me through a grove of grown-ups in the kitchen, people holding cups of tea and biscuit-bearing saucers parting to let us through. I couldn't see the daybed. I wondered if Murchie was underneath it or whether it had been moved somewhere else. If the former, he'd be surprised and perhaps terrified by all the commotion just beyond the blanket. I imagined him under there, his yellow eyes even wider than usual as he cowered in the corner.

It was likewise crowded in the dim hallway that led past Ned and Lucy's room to the Shrine Room, where the light was not on and the curtains were drawn as always. Those few who were speaking were doing so in hushed and solemn tones. Lucy lay in the bed, her head sideways on a pillow, her eyes closed. Ned and Father McGettigan sat side by side on kitchen chairs, my aunts and uncles gathered around them. Jennie led me to the other side of the bed, away from the crowd. Lucy was paler than I'd ever seen her, which made her eyebrows seem even darker.

Jennie crouched down so that her mouth was at Lucy's ear. "Wayne is here. Wayne is here to see you."

Lucy opened her eyes. Jennie moved me slightly closer to the bed and into Lucy's line of sight. "I'm a sick woman, Wayne," Lucy said.

"I know," was all I could think of to say.

She managed to shift her head so that she could see the Shrine, the statue of Mary with Baby Jesus in her arms, the blue, frosted votive candle in front of it, the flame inside unlit.

"We spent a lot of time in front of the Shrine, didn't we, Wayne?" she said. I nodded and looked at the framed photographs displayed at Mary's feet. "I'll be with Leonard soon," Lucy said. I looked at the picture of Ned and Leonard in the hayfield. Though the picture was black and white, you could tell that the day had been not only sunny but very warm. But Leonard was dressed in layers of clothes as though for late fall.

I glanced at Ned, who was listening to something the priest was saying to him. He didn't seem sad. Unlike most of the others, who were dressed as though for church, he was wearing denim overalls, his massive arms folded across them.

"We said a lot of prayers to Mary, didn't we, Wayne?" Lucy said. Feeling guilty, I nodded again. I hadn't really prayed for Lucy, and here she was, sick, expecting to be with Leonard soon.

"Give me a hug," she said.

Using my one good arm for balance on the bed, I tried to press my head against her shoulder so she could reach me. I might have fallen on top of her if not for Jennie, who took hold of my shoulders from behind. Lucy smiled wanly and closed her eyes. Then she opened them again and said, "Why don't you light the candle?"

"Here," Jennie said, extending to me her Bic cigarette lighter. I took it with my shaking right hand and managed to turn the little wheel with my thumb and produce a flame on the second try. When I turned the lighter upside down to hold the flame to the wick, I burned my thumb and forefinger. Thankfully, the wick caught, and I hastily withdrew my hand.

"Let's say a prayer to Mary and the Baby Jesus." Lucy closed her eyes again and I closed mine, too, but I could think of nothing but my thumb and finger, which stung so much that tears seeped out from beneath my eyelids. I heard a collective indrawing of breath around us, several loud sobs and others that were partially stifled. I opened my eyes, but Lucy's were still closed.

"All right," Jennie whispered, "we'll go now." She led me out of the room through the vigil keepers, wiping away both her tears and mine.

Once we were back at the house, Jennie gave me a fierce hug, then turned and hurried back out the door, her hand over her mouth, her body stooped forward as if her legs might give way.

Throughout it all, the two quarters, the dime and the nickel I stole from Dad's pants had been in my pocket, clinking occasionally. I wondered where I should hide them.

Two weeks after my deathbed visit—two weeks during which Dad stayed home from work with us and didn't go again to the Crystal—Lucy was up and about.

It was widely believed that I had prayed that she wouldn't

die, and my prayer was answered. My lighting of the candle, my silent prayer, my tears, were the talk of the Goulds.

"It was Wayne who brought her back," Dot Chafe told Jennie on the phone, and this, or some version of it, became the consensus. God had answered the prayer of Lucy's weeping grandson just after he lit a candle for her in front of Mary and the Baby Jesus. Jennie's boy, looking as though he was not much further from death's door than Lucy was, had been called for and led into the Shrine Room, where, crying tears of sorrow for the grandmother with whom he was known to be so close, he offered up a votive prayer to God that she not be taken from him. And she wasn't.

I was told that Father McGettigan—though he discouraged the word "miracle"—believed that what he and the others had witnessed demonstrated the reach and power of God's Grace and that the person he had chosen to be the instrument of that Grace had been, in the typical, classical Christian manner, not only a child, but one who had endured more without complaint than most people managed to struggle through in a lifetime.

I felt guilty, selfish, foolish—but I was so glad that Lucy had recovered that these feelings went away.

I soon resumed my routine of spending the day with Lucy, who told me that, while I should not let what people were saying go to my head, she, too, believed that, had I not lit the candle and prayed for her, she would have been a goner.

Over a game of cards, she said that she had had Last Rites and that there was a man, John Howlett, who was going around saying that what she had been given must have been Next-to-Last Rites. He was calling her all sorts of things, including False Alarm Lucy, and Lucy Lazarus, and saying that she had gotten people's hopes up for nothing and that he wouldn't pal around with someone who had been resurrected from the dead. "Smart arse. He's making a big joke of it."

She said it wasn't her who called for the priest but Dr. McIntyre. "That doctor being what he is, there might be a lot of false alarms. By the time I do go, people will be so fed up there'll be no one there to say goodbye."

At last, I was able to tell her about the Crystal and the things Dad had said, dwelling longest on the words I couldn't get out of my head—*more trouble than the other three combined.*

"Dad said he'd be some kind of bigshot if not for us."

"What does he think he would be?"

"A scientist, I think. A Master of science."

"A scientist. A *Master* of science, no less. Maybe someone told him that the instructions for how to become a scientist are written on the bottom of a beer bottle, but they forgot to tell him which one. Don't tell him I said that or I'll be in more trouble than the *six* of you combined."

"I won't tell," I said.

"That's what he was up to while your mother was over here with me—he was drinking beer at the Crystal along with all the other scientists?"

I nodded.

Lucy said she was glad that Jennie hadn't left *her* in the back seat of a car in the parking lot of the Crystal while she went in for a quick break from taking care of her.

She had yet to hear of youngsters roaming around the Crystal, telling waitresses they were trying to find their *mother* who had pulled a fast one on them so that she could spend the rent and get on the nerves of all the other mothers who were taking a quick break from keeping their children alive, only to have it ruined by a recitation of the dreams that had been thwarted by her family.

After cards, we went down the hall and knelt at the Shrine.

"It's strange, isn't it?" she said, looking around. "This room was full of people snottin' and bawlin' and here I am, as good as new. You never know which way things will go, do you?"

"No," I said.

She was silent for a while, then said, "I thought about being a nun, you know."

"Did you?"

"Oh yes. That was another false alarm, I suppose. There's no sacrament that makes you a nun. The sacrament that makes you a priest is called Holy Orders. A priest is like a doctor and a nun is like a nurse. I suppose any woman can learn how to be a nun. I went to school with some of the nuns at St. Kevin's. There wasn't one called Sister Einstein, I can tell you that. But some of them were smart enough. I never finished school, never even came close, so who am I to talk?"

She fell silent again, then lit the votive candle and blew out the match.

"I wasn't afraid the day you came to see me," she said. "Not one bit, not after I got Last Rites." She welled up. "I thought about my little boy. I kept thinking I would see him any second. He would have his mother again, any second. He wouldn't be by himself."

twenty

It was so long since Dr. McIntyre had threatened to report Jennie and Dad for neglect that I had almost come to think that welfare officers were bogeymen that grown-ups in positions of authority had invented to keep other grown-ups in line. When the phone call that Jennie lived in fear of came at last, I was as surprised as I would have been if Santa Claus had called to say that he'd been receiving so many reports about me misbehaving that he planned to stop by the house unannounced to see if they were true.

It may have been Dr. McIntyre who turned us in. Someone who knew about the Saturday afternoon scene at the Crystal may have told him that the four Johnston boys had been abandoned in the family car by their father and had gone inside the bar to find him, which resulted in a near brawl and the humiliating expulsion of all five of the Johnston males.

When Jennie got off the phone that evening in mid-February, she looked more taken aback than I had ever seen her. I doubt that a slap in the face would have shocked her as much. Her chin wobbled for a bit as if she were about to cry, but then she recovered and said there was a woman coming to the house in an hour to see if there was anything that she could help us with. We boys were to put on our best clothes and tidy up the bunk room while she and Dad tidied up the rest of the house.

Here was the greatest shame that could befall a family—we had been deemed unfit to take care of ourselves. The authorities had had to intervene. Jennie likely believed that she was looked upon as being especially derelict. The mother. The wife. The moral centre of the household. Men and boys would be men and boys, but Jennie Johnston was deemed to have fallen below the standard of decent, capable women. She had failed.

We boys waited in the bunk room, dressed and scrubbed as if for church, standing so as not to wrinkle our clothes, the four of us scared into silence until my cough started up.

At last, we heard a car pull into the driveway. The car, I thought, that Dr. McIntyre had warned Jennie about, the one that all her neighbours would see, conspicuously, blatantly, shamefully *there*. I wondered what it looked like.

The doorbell rang—until that moment, I didn't know we had one. I heard Jennie walk at what she must have hoped would sound like a casual pace to the front door. She opened it and said, in an attempt at a breezy, cordial tone that was so overdone it was ghastly, "Come right in, ma'am." I couldn't make out the woman's reply, nor the brief exchange between her and Jennie as they made their way to the kitchen.

I briefly heard Dad's voice, then the woman speaking at length, the scraping of a chair on the kitchen floor and, shortly after, two knocks on the bunk room door.

"Wayne," Jennie called through the door, "Mrs. Densmore would like to meet you."

"Surprise, surprise," Craig muttered.

I opened the door and looked up at Jennie, whose lips were pressed into a thin line. She took me by the hand, led me out and closed the door. We walked hand in hand to the kitchen, where she manoeuvred me in front of her and gently guided me across the room to the table.

Mrs. Densmore, whose back was to me, turned about in her chair and smiled. "This must be Wayne," she said as my mother moved me to the empty chair opposite her.

"Say hello," Jennie said, forcing a laugh as if to say that here I was again, remaining silent upon meeting a woman who had come to see if there was anything that she could help us with.

Mrs. Densmore was still wearing her coat, which was buttoned to the neck. She had curly, greying hair. Her cheeks were flushed as if she was nervous.

"Hello," I said, taking a seat. When our eyes met, her face fell as if I looked worse than someone had led her to expect. She was holding a pen, and a clipboard bearing a yellow notepad lay on the table in front of her. I glanced at Dad, whose eyes, as he stubbed out a cigarette, were downcast.

Mrs. Densmore, in a voice that failed offhandedness as badly as Jennie's had, said that, as she'd been telling my parents, this was mainly a get-to-know-you visit. She said it as if, even as she spoke, women like her were stopping in on families all over the Goulds to get to know them and to see if there was anything they could do to help them.

I'd been seeing a lot of doctors lately?

"Yes."

Did I know why?

"I'm always sick. I might have a murmur and a worm."

"A heart murmur and a tapeworm," Jennie said. "He *has* a heart murmur, but we still don't know how serious it is. The stomach doctor said he doesn't think Wayne has a tapeworm. We're waiting on some other doctors to rule things out."

As Jennie spoke, Mrs. Densmore remained focused on me. She consulted her notepad. "You may have pleurisy. Possibly something else. You're malnourished. Very short and small for your age. You can't sleep because you cough when you lie down. You're often fatigued, probably because you don't get enough sleep."

"I *try* to sleep in the bedmobile," I said. "But, even when I don't cough, I can't sleep."

Mrs. Densmore raised her eyebrows. "The bedmobile?"

"It's a little bed with wheels on it so you can move it around. My brothers won't let me sleep in their room because I cough so much I keep them awake."

"So where do you sleep?"

"Wherever I put the bedmobile. Mostly in the living room. Sometimes in the dining room. Sometimes here."

"In the kitchen?"

I nodded.

"So you don't have a bedroom?"

"He stays in the bunk room with the other boys sometimes," Jennie said. "That's where his clothes are."

"That's a strange arrangement."

"It's only temporary," Jennie said. "Until his cough gets better."

"What's your favourite food, Wayne?" Mrs. Densmore said.

"Fried potatoes. But I don't feel like eating anything most of the time."

"His eyes are bigger than his belly," Jennie said.

"Lucy says a mosquito's eyes are bigger than my belly."

"Lucy is his grandmother," Jennie said. "What happens is, he eats so much he makes himself sick."

"Even a little bit makes me sick," I said. Jennie frowned.

"You have some broken teeth," Mrs. Densmore said. "What happened?"

"I got dizzy from a fever. They filled the tub with ice but I was still too warm."

"Oh my, that must have been awful. Can you smile so that I can see your teeth?"

Instead of smiling, I used the thumb of my good hand to raise my upper lip. Mrs. Densmore winced.

"They're infected," she said. "There's at least one abscess I can see."

"Yes, ma'am," Jennie said.

Mrs. Densmore turned to her. "Has Wayne been taking the various medications that he's been prescribed? Has he been to see a physiotherapist about his arm?"

Jennie said not as such. She hadn't had time to take me to a physiotherapist, what with Lucy being sick. She hadn't filled the prescriptions yet because the drugs were a bit expensive. "But I have money coming."

Where was it coming from and when? Mrs. Densmore asked.

From a relative on the mainland. Very soon. As if the arrival at our house of money from the mainland, where, as she didn't doubt Mrs. Densmore knew, it grew on trees, was always imminent.

"Wayne has to have those medications *very* soon."

"Yes, ma'am. I have money coming. It got held up, but now it's coming."

"Child Welfare can help you pay for the medications," Mrs. Densmore said.

Jennie insisted that there wouldn't be any need for that because of the money that was coming from the mainland. It would be here any day now. Surely Mrs. Densmore knew that even money from the mainland could be delayed.

"Well, I hope so. Wayne's teeth—an abscess can be very serious. Antibiotics aren't all *that* expensive."

"I didn't know about the abscess. It must have just started."

"It looks very painful, not like it just started. He didn't say anything about it?"

"No, ma'am. Not as such."

Mrs. Densmore looked at me. I didn't know what to say because I had no idea what an abscess was or when mine had started.

"He should get antibiotics for that right away. Tomorrow. I can give you something to give the pharmacist—"

"I have enough for that," Jennie said. "I didn't know about the abscess. Now that I know, it won't be a problem."

"Well, I hope not," Mrs. Densmore said. "You'll have to see a doctor first to get a prescription. Or I could get one for you from Dr. McIntyre and give it to the pharmacist. I think that would be the best thing, don't you?"

"That's all right, ma'am," Jennie said. "We can take Wayne to a doctor in town. The one we used to go to when we lived there. We know him better. Wayne likes him. And we know the druggist there, near where we lived. I was going to town tomorrow anyway, so . . ."

"Well—all right then, if you're sure."

"I'm sure. And I have money coming."

I felt relieved. I was as loath to see Dr. McIntyre as Jennie obviously was. And she didn't want Mrs. Densmore dropping off a prescription for me at the drugstore in the Goulds because the pharmacist would tell everyone.

"I'll be back to see you and your parents very soon, Wayne," Mrs. Densmore said to me.

"I have three brothers," I said. "One of them is younger than me."

"I'll meet them next time." Mrs. Densmore stood, bade us goodbye and said she could see herself out, which she did, her expression blank, the redness in her cheeks that I had taken as a sign of nervousness still there.

The instant the front door closed, Jennie, who hadn't smoked during Mrs. Densmore's visit, took one from Dad's pack and lit it. She pressed the fingertips of her free hand so hard against her forehead that they turned bright red. Her eyes welled up and her cigarette hand shook.

"She'll be back tomorrow night," she said, "to check about those antibiotics."

"I can borrow a few bucks from someone at work," Dad said.

My brothers came out of the bunk room and stood around the table.

"Are we moving again?" Brian said.

Jennie shook her head and managed to smile at him. "She's been assigned to us. We're part of her caseload. Viola Densmore. I know her people. They're from Petty Harbour. They're piss-poor, all of them, her parents, her brothers and sisters. *They're* probably part of someone's caseload. I wouldn't be surprised if *she* was. She was when she was growing up. Or maybe her family is part of *her* caseload. There used to be about forty-five of them under one roof. Her mother had to do a roll call every night at bedtime. 'Possibly something else,' she said because she couldn't pronounce 'pulmonary fibrosis.' And now *she's* the one judging me? Viola Densmore?"

"You shouldn't have told her you have money coming," Dad said.

"We'll probably never see her again after tomorrow night," Jennie said. "Not a cent are we taking from welfare."

"Jennie—" Dad began.

"She sized *you* up pretty fast, I'll give her that," Jennie said. "*Do you take a drink now and then, Mr. Johnston?* Butter wouldn't melt in her mouth. I should have told her Wayne wouldn't get tipsy from the beer that's left over in Newfoundland by the time her father passes out from drinking. *And you have another one on the way, is that right, Mrs. Johnston?* I should have said yes, the youngsters just keep coming. I'm as puzzled about how that happens as your mother was."

She looked at me. "Why didn't you tell me about that abscess?"

"I didn't know about it." But I felt it, now, throbbing in time with my heartbeat.

Dad said this was all his fault. No wonder Child Welfare was on our doorstep. His own boys had to come into the Crystal because he left them outside in the car after promising to drive them up the Shore.

"I'm no good and I never was. It's just as well to face facts. What kind of man would do something like that? I'm the reason that woman is hounding us . . ."

Jennie listened in silence as he went on and on, long enough for him to give himself the dressing-down that he deserved. Then she finally interrupted him, told him he was being too hard on himself, not giving himself nearly the credit he deserved. He was a good man but a flawed one and she wasn't going to sit there while he tore himself down in front of us children. By the time she was done, all four of us boys were endorsing her every word, castigating him for not appreciating just how fine a man he was, while he sat there and took it all in, his expression saying that if the only way to keep the peace was to allow us to esteem him too highly, then so be it.

No one ripped into anyone, despite Mrs. Densmore. We went to the doctor in town the next day and got a prescription for penicillin, which Dad borrowed the money to pay for.

twenty-one

"I suppose she means well," Lucy said the next day. "The problem with giving people two dollars is that it makes them feel like two cents. I'd rather be on welfare than be a welfare officer. You should see the kind of places they send them to. Well, I guess you've seen more than one, haven't you? But a gun and a badge would come in handy at most places. I knew a woman who had twenty-three children, all by Caesarean section."

"Dad said he knew a woman who had twenty-*one* children the same way."

"It was twenty-three," Lucy snapped. "Her and her mister had to get the priest involved, and he got the bishop involved, and it all wound up on the pope's desk. He gave them permission to stay clear of each other until she was too old to have another youngster. That was in the paper, so don't think I'm making it up. Your mother is right about Viola Densmore, the poor woman. You can't get a better expert on child poverty than someone who spent their childhood fighting off dogs to get first crack at a bone that wasn't fit for making soup."

She suggested we go to the Shrine and light the candle and pray to Mary and the Baby Jesus to make Viola Densmore too busy to bother with us. We knelt in front of the statue and she lit the candle.

"May is Mary's month. You and I were born in May. If you ever feel like it's all getting to be too much for you, you should pray to Mary. It doesn't have to be here at the Shrine. It could be anywhere."

"Sometimes I think it *is* all too much for me," I said.

"What?" she said. "I meant you should pray to Mary when you're my age and it's all too much for you. I've never known a youngster your age to be such a worrywart. Are you worried about being sick or are you sick because you're worried?"

"I don't know."

"What are you worried about?"

"I might be like Leonard. I might die."

"You don't have to worry about dying, my love, because you're definitely going to. If you're trying to figure out a way to live forever, no wonder you don't sleep."

"I worry about other things, too."

"Like what?"

"Like are we going to move again."

"From what I've seen, that's as certain as death, so I wouldn't worry about that, either. What else?"

"Dad spending the rent and Mom ripping into him."

"Do you ever worry about anything that *isn't* a sure bet?"

"Like what?"

"Like who's going to win the hockey game."

"What about my arm?"

"What about it? Worry won't fix it."

"Maybe nothing will."

"Maybe. But worry definitely won't."

She fell into one of the silences that I was becoming accustomed to.

"You know," she said at last, "the name Lucy is a bit too much like Lucifer. He got off to a good start, just like you. He brought Light into the darkness of the Deep. Lucifer the Light Bringer, that's what he was called. Maybe that's why I like to light this candle. But then he went and got too big for his boots. He got all full of himself and how he was as great as God. Soon, there was a whole bunch of backstabbers out to get the Lord Almighty. Some don't know how good they have it. Runner-up to God and still he wanted more. Him and his archangel friends, they shagged it all up. You're not exactly an archangel, what with the size of you and all your troubles, but you have more sense than to pick a fight with God."

I had no idea until the next day why Lucy had given me such an odd compliment. Just after Ned left the house to go back to work after lunch, Father McGettigan stopped by. I could tell by Lucy's lack of surprise and only moderate nervousness that she had been expecting him. He was dressed in black but for his white collar, a man of middle height and greying hair.

His high-pitched voice had often inspired Dad to imitate the way he sang the Latin portions of the Mass, and I'd many times interrupted Father McGettigan by breaking out into a fit of coughing that caused Jennie to lead me from church.

"Hello, Wayne," he said, as Lucy led him from the front door to where I was sitting at the end of the table in the kitchen. The two of them sat as well, McGettigan at right angles to me, Lucy at the other end.

"Hello, Father," I said. This was the closest I'd ever been to him except in the confessional.

He said that I was far too young to decide about the proposal he had come to make. He was aware of my tribulations, my various health concerns and the way they set me apart from other boys my age, and even from my own brothers, who were not without tribulations of their own. But mine, he said, were sometimes a sign that God had chosen a child to lead a special kind of life. Lucy had told him of our daily visits to the Shrine of the Blessed Virgin and the Baby Jesus, the lighting of the votive candle and the prayers we said together. He said it was rare for a young boy to be so devout, as it was for one to be tested as I had been and to come through it without complaint, dimming of spirit or loss of innocence. He said that time would tell if God had chosen and prepared me for a life apart, a difficult but profoundly rewarding life of service to the Church, to the Body of Christ, to the priesthood. He had heard from Sister Paschal that I was very bright, "exceptional" was the word she used, a quality that would serve me well in the seminary, if I chose the priesthood. But all this was far down the road and more in God's hands than his or mine.

In the meantime, he said, he wondered if I would like to become an altar boy, if not right away, then when my health improved, which, God willing, it would soon. At any rate, I should remember that physical imperfections need not deter me from a life of service—on the contrary, some of the greatest of the Church Fathers and many of the saints had, by the weaknesses of their bodies, been inspired to a level of spirituality and acts of self-sacrifice far beyond the scope of their able-bodied counterparts.

Shortly after, he bade me good afternoon with a final smile and left. After Lucy walked him to the front door, she came back to where I was sitting in front of a cup of tea I hadn't touched.

"Well," she said, "I liked that visit to my house a lot more than the last one he made."

Who had first proposed the idea, I wondered, him or her? She must have seen the question in my eyes.

"He saw you when you came to say goodbye to me," she said. "He said he was struck by how you carried yourself. He said you seemed much older than you are."

"He seemed nice," I said.

"Well," she said, "it's no odds if nothing more comes of it. Most people never get singled out for anything."

That night, over supper, I told everyone about it. Jennie looked distressed, but before she could say a word, Ken and Craig started in about whether or not it would be possible for someone with as many things wrong with him as I had to become a priest.

"Only one of your arms works," Craig said, "and it's not the one you used to use the most. How could you hold the thurible?"

"He could raise the chalice with one hand," Ken said.

I pictured myself holding up the chalice in the triumphant pose of a trophy winner.

"How would you hold up the Host?" Craig said. "You have to hold a piece in each hand. And you have to eat it and keep it down, not spit it all over the altar."

"All you ever do in church is cough," Ken said. "A priest has to *say* the Mass, not cough it. Some parts you'd have to sing."

"Yeah," Craig said, "but Jennie wouldn't have to send Dad to Mass in a storm anymore because Wayne could say Mass at home."

"Stop it, boys," Jennie said.

"It would be just as hard for him to be an altar boy as a priest," Craig said. "I suppose he could ring the angelus bells with one hand and cough out the candles."

Dad, imitating Father McGettigan's squeaky voice, said, "The Pharisees and the Hennesseys."

All of us but Jennie laughed. "Stop it!" she said, and Ken and Craig suddenly looked sheepish because Jennie had started crying.

"*Another* thing to worry about," she said. "It's not enough for him to get better—he has to be a *priest*? Now Father McGettigan will have his eyes on us, too. He might even come by the house. Dr. McIntyre, Viola Densmore, now Father McGettigan. Who will it be next?"

She looked at me as if to say, "Will you ever stop making things worse?"

"And this will cost *more* money. An altar boy's uniform costs a fortune."

"Maybe the Church pays for it," Craig said.

Dad said it was the parishioners who paid for the Church.

Jennie said what if the priest and Viola Densmore started comparing notes.

Dad said I didn't have to be an altar boy, let alone a priest, if I didn't want to. Father McGettigan was the least of our worries.

Jennie said that, what with her mother having had such a close call and still not having fully recovered, and what with Viola Densmore snooping around, and what with them still waiting to hear if I would need an operation and have to go to Montreal to have it, and still waiting to hear if the lung man had ruled out *his* disease, not to mention all the medications I needed that they couldn't afford, me being singled out by Father McGettigan to be a priest was the absolute, very last straw.

Two evenings later, Ken came out of the bathroom to say that the toilet was stogged. He'd tried for ten minutes to unstog it with a plunger, with no success.

After accusing Ken of using too much toilet paper, Dad also tried the plunger. Then he poured a bucket of water into the bowl but it didn't go down and the toilet almost overflowed.

Jennie put down the toilet cover and said we should wait a while to see if the water went down on its own. It didn't. Dad said we would have to get a plumber, but Jennie said we couldn't afford one, unless he planned to do what he always did when something broke down and hire someone who would make things worse because his only qualification was that he *called* himself a plumber.

Dad took the phone book to the kitchen table and flipped through the yellow pages. He found the number of a plumber who would come to the house and give an estimate for no charge.

The man showed up quickly, examined the pipes in the unfinished basement and declared them to be blocked their entire length, probably because the septic tank was full—it would need to be dug up and emptied or replaced.

After he'd gone, Jennie ripped into Dad. Because of him, we never had a margin for error, but that was like being on easy street compared to this. Because of him, we'd never been able to save a cent for a rainy day, and we had never had a day rainier than this one. She kept at him until he declared himself to be less than worthless. He had to continue in this vein for far longer than usual before she relented and told him that it was him who, in a way that not everyone was able to appreciate, kept the Johnstons on course during times when other families would have lost their way. Looking at us children, she said that if we could see into the houses of the men at the Crystal, we would know what true worthlessness looked like and how much more decent a man Dad was than those who put on a better show.

We were silent until Jennie, though sounding more collected, said, "So what are we going to *do*?" We couldn't complain to the landlord because he would say it was our fault, and there would go our rent deposit, and more. Dad said he bet the landlord knew that the tank was nearly full when we moved in.

Jennie said there were the bathrooms at school for three of the boys, during the day at least, and the one across the road at Lucy's when Wayne was over there. There were bathrooms where Dad worked. Then Dad asked what about her and what about the rest of the time?

"Maybe we could use Ned's outhouse," I said.

It was a few feet to one side of the barn. Although he and Lucy had had indoor plumbing for years, he used this shed-sized outhouse instead because he was convinced that it was unseemly and unhygienic to go to the bathroom in the place in which you slept and ate and had guests, in which your every bathroom noise could be overheard. In which odours would linger and germs would spread. He thought it more decorous, more private and, health-wise, more sensible to keep separate the house in which you lived and the place in which you used the bathroom.

Dad said that Ned would either say no or he'd say yes, but people would find out and we'd never hear the end of it.

"If Viola Densmore found out," Jennie said, glancing at me. "If she knew that Wayne was going over there at night, in the dark, in the winter, with nowhere to wash his hands."

I wondered just how close I really was to winding up in some foster home.

"Of all the things that could go wrong *now*," Dad said.

We were silent again until Jennie said, "I'll give Lucy a call."

"I'll use the woods before I accept one more thing from her," Dad said. "We all should."

Yes, Jennie said, and how would that look come spring, when the snow was gone? A nice sight for the people of Petty Harbour Road, toilet tissue popping up like blossoms on the floor of the woods behind our house, the woods dotted all over with a winter's worth of soiled toilet tissue. And what about when the days got longer? How would we keep our secret then?

❧

"So this is the arrangement," Jennie said after talking to her mother. "She says Wayne and I can use the indoor bathroom, even at night, and the rest of you can use the outhouse whenever you like."

"I told you I'd rather go out in the woods behind the house," Dad said.

"No one is using the woods," Jennie said. "Lucy will leave the side door light on for Wayne and me. The rest of you will have to use a flashlight, like Ned does. There's no light in the outhouse. You'll have to be as quiet as a mouse, Wayne, even when Ned is still up."

"I might cough," I said. I was certain that I would.

"Lucy said she knows that can't be helped."

Craig said that, as always, I was getting special treatment.

"Your brother is *sick*," Jennie said. "It's bad enough that he'll have to go out into the cold at night. Lucy said she couldn't have the whole family traipsing through her house at all hours. Now, for God's sake, no one say a word about this to anyone."

The next day, during my jug bath, Lucy also told me not to say a word to anyone, especially not to Ned. "Not that the two of you are in the habit of sitting down together and having long discussions, but I'm reminding you, just in case. He's not too happy about the whole arrangement, and anything might set him off. He said he knew an indoor toilet wouldn't last kissing time and he's never known why he should be the one to pay for what other people are foolish enough to fall for. I don't know what he'll do with the toilet if I die first because *he'll* never have a visitor. Fill it up with earth and plant flowers in it, maybe. Or keep the lid down and put knick-knacks on it. Make it look like a piece of furniture. Paint it a different colour than the sink and tub."

I thought about Ned taking a bath beside a purely decorative toilet, just as my family and I would be doing until we could afford to have ours fixed.

"Aside from this house, that outhouse is the last thing left from what he built when he started the farm—he wouldn't be delighted if the whole thing went up in flames one night because of where your father dropped a cigarette. He won't mind you and Jennie coming and going. He was well used to our youngsters getting up at all hours to go out before we got the indoor bathroom. The sound of a door opening and closing won't bother either one of us. I wasn't about to have Jennie, five or six months along, catching her death in that place, or you for that matter—you'd have pneumonia in a week. I know what using an outhouse is like. At least your father and your brothers won't have to use newspaper and wind up with head-lines on their backsides. It'll be a long winter for the lot of you, living on one side of the road and doing your business on the other. Ned says the weather will be rough for a while. Lots of snow, he says, and then a cold spell. He's usually right. I've never known a family to have such bad luck with houses, but this takes the cake."

twenty-two

As I was mostly awake throughout the night, I often watched from my bed in the living room as Jennie, Dad or one of my brothers came out to the vestibule to put on their winter coats, boots, caps and mitts before making their way out into the cold and across the road to Lucy's, or to Ned's outhouse.

As Ned had predicted, it soon turned bitterly cold and there were frequent snowstorms, the wind shaking the house, piling the snow into drifts in the driveway, on the road and in Ned and Lucy's yard.

On the worst nights, Jennie woke Dad so that he could walk Brian across the road to the outhouse and wait outside until he emerged again. Dad *always* accompanied me, because of my arm—Jennie was terrified I'd lose my balance and hit my head on the ice. I was more afraid of getting stuck in the snow and needing Dad to drag me out. Through a series of contortions impossible to describe, I was now able to manage all of my clothing, so, to my great relief, Dad did not have to help me pull my pants up.

I watched through the curtains as various members of my family fought the snow and wind, flashlight in hand, the bobbing of the light sometimes the only thing I could make out. When they came back, they were red-faced with cold, shaking the snow off their mitts, stamping the warmth back into their feet.

Jennie always made the trip by herself, presumably out of some combination of modesty and self-reliance, but she and I had the luxury of warming up in Lucy's house before heading back across the road.

The others rarely spoke to me, coming or going, but Craig always had something to say to me while he put on or took off his outer clothes. Sometimes he merely said, "Jennie's boy." Or he asked me why I didn't simply live at Lucy's, given how much time I spent there. He said I had two mothers, but he and Ken and Brian had none because of how much time Jennie and Lucy spent with me. Couldn't I go to sleep so that the rest of them didn't have the added embarrassment of being watched? He said they would soon find out who had stogged up the toilet if Lucy's got stogged up, and it wouldn't be Jennie. Then I would really be in trouble, two stogged-up toilets on my rap sheet. He said it was just as well I didn't use the outhouse because I was so small I would probably slide straight in. On the other hand, that was something he wouldn't mind seeing, though it might be even better to see how I'd get out and what I looked like when I did.

One evening, at the dinner table, Craig said, "Tonight, I'm going into the inside bathroom. How will they know the difference?"

"Me, too," Brian said.

"Don't you dare," Jennie said. "If you get caught, none of us will have *any*where to go. And then we'd have nowhere to live. We'd wind up living on the street."

"I've never seen a single family living *on* the street," Craig said.

"It's just an expression," Jennie said.

"For what?" Craig asked.

"You wouldn't want to know."

"We haven't even got a street," Craig said. "We have a road and nobody lives *on* it. Even if there was no traffic, why would they?"

"So help me God," Jennie said, "if one of you goes into Lucy's pretending to be Wayne—"

"If I ever pretend to be someone else, it won't be Wayne," Craig said.

Jennie said we were lucky we didn't have neighbours close by. They would have figured out what was going on by now and word would have gotten back to Viola Densmore.

Craig said Mrs. Densmore wouldn't care if it wasn't for me. The Johnstons wouldn't be part of her caseload if not for me. But then he got up and walked over to me and tousled my hair in a way that, though meant to bolster my spirits, made it all too clear how glad he was that he was not living my life.

❧

It sometimes seemed strange and sometimes entirely unremarkable, this nighttime staggered trek of my family from one side of the road to the other, each of us with toilet paper folded in our pockets, a flashlight in our hands, one part of the family headed for a frigid outhouse, the other for an indoor bathroom but still having to endure the trip there and back, the numbing cold, the obstacle course of snowdrifts.

I fancied that Dad and I looked strangest of all, walking side by side, him holding the flashlight and me my bamboo cane, two mismatched companions on an absurd but urgent mission, heads tucked, bird-wise, into our shoulders to shield our faces from the slant, skin-drilling snow.

Dad swore from one side of the road to the other, either at himself or whatever forces he chose on any given night to accuse of conspiring to reduce him to spending his nights this way.

Of all the ridiculous predicaments a man could find himself in, this covert nightly foray into the outdoors from a rented house with an unworkable toilet to the house owned by his backward-thinking, primitive in-laws, who not only owned their house outright but also had an outhouse that his father-in-law preferred to a modern, working bathroom, had to be the most ridiculous and most humiliating.

Aside from having to escort me, he said, he had to undertake his own journey so that he could squat in the same sort of structure he had grown up squatting in, finding his way by flashlight, plunking himself down on the very circle of wood that his wife and her siblings had sat on as children, the very one his mother-in-law had availed herself of for years on end. The one his father-in-law still used.

While he waited for me, he had to stand outside in the cold, hidden from the road, from pedestrians or people in passing cars, who, Jennie kept warning him, would somehow (how?) guess his reason for being there, stamping his feet, smoking a cigarette, passing the time as best he could while, inside, the most sickly of his children dawdled about in the warmth of a modern, functioning bathroom such as the universe had deemed must be withheld from him.

On the orders of his wife, he could not even wait in the side porch lest he be seen through the window or be happened upon by one or both of her parents, which, she seemed to think, would magnify her own shame far beyond his.

He likewise waited outside on the stormiest nights for Brian. Watching through the curtains while kneeling on the chesterfield, I saw them cross the road, Brian clinging to Dad's hand as they struggled through the deep snow.

I watched them all, Craig plodding furiously across the road, his hands in his pockets—he disdained the flashlight—shoulders hunched as he kicked aside pieces of ice like a football punter, so exasperated was he, so furious that he, who prided himself on never looking foolish, never playing chump to the wise guys of the world, should have no choice but to do *this* night after night.

I watched Ken plow through the snow with his long legs, forever adjusting his glasses, seemingly unworried about being seen, as if he was so well used to the tribulations of the Johnstons he assumed that others were as well and would therefore make nothing of this latest one.

It was when I watched Jennie make the journey to her parents' house that I felt the greatest pangs of guilt, my pregnant mother, having left home so many years ago, now having come full circle with no choice but to accept their charity in this strangest and most humiliating of ways.

I watched my mother nimbly make her way over the top of the snow, which, however new, did not give way beneath her, my mother pregnant with her fifth child but gamely determined to somehow make it through this family fiasco or even turn our luck around so that we could begin the long climb back up the social ladder to the rung she'd imagined she'd reach when she married the first educated man she'd ever met, the husband who could not put aside the notion that he was a better man by far than he was thought to be.

She climbed the steps of the side porch as she must have done hundreds of times in her youth, entered the house she knew every inch of by heart and, minutes later, emerged and, likely knowing I was watching, made her way to the road she had grown up by, the one that, for a time, she thought she would look back on as the place of her humble beginnings.

twenty-three

I was at Lucy's, in the kitchen, about to go with her to light the votive candle, when the phone rang. She answered it, but was gone only a minute. When she came back, she said that Jennie had called. She had just heard from Dr. Barton, the heart man, whose colleague on the mainland had confirmed that my heart murmur was benign. On behalf of the lung man, he also confirmed that I didn't have the fibrosis thing, either, but I did have pleurisy. There would be no need for a trip to Montreal, no murmur surgery.

Lucy gave me a hug and said, "Jennie is so relieved she's crying her eyes out. Why don't you run across the road to see her? Remember I told you not to fret about that murmur?"

When I got home, Jennie gave me a fiercer and longer hug than Lucy had. She was still crying when she phoned Dad at work. I was relieved, too, though my belief in the reality of Montreal had been on a par with my belief in the reality of the future. I still couldn't imagine it, didn't believe in it or in things as nebulous as adulthood, marriage or parenthood. That a heart murmur or anything else was harmless was as good as saying it did not exist.

Dad came home from work that night with several paper bags containing bottles of pills, capsules, tablets and a large green bottle of what Jennie said was syrup to rid me of the tapeworm that Dr. Hayward was almost sure I didn't have. The other medications were for my pleurisy, except for one that was a refill of penicillin—I had another abscess, and Dr. Barton had told Jennie I would go on getting abscesses until my teeth were fixed.

The bad news, which Jennie held back until Dad got home, was that physiotherapy would do my arm no good. We'd just have to wait to see if it healed.

Dad, who'd been drinking, but not a lot, as far as I could tell, said that what doctors got away with was criminal. McIntyre had ruined my life and hadn't so much as apologized.

I didn't like to think of myself as ruined but, despite Jennie's objections that we should be happy because the worst of my problems had been resolved, Dad was soon going on about everything I would miss out on. I'd never go fishing again or play hockey or baseball or other sports.

Craig said that McIntyre may have done damage to the nerve in my arm, but he had done none to my chances of becoming an all-round athlete.

How would I drive a car or do other things that people took for granted? Dad asked. Jennie was still cutting up my food.

I had learned to write almost as well with my right hand as I had with my left and hadn't really considered the possibility before that my arm would never get better.

But, Craig said, I had a fallback plan. I could be a priest.

Of the medicine Dad had brought home, I was to take one capsule and one tablet at mealtimes for two weeks for my pleurisy and two teaspoons of the tapeworm medicine each night. The pills went down easily enough. The syrup, which was strawberry-flavoured and momentarily soothing, made me burp—it was supposed to, Jennie said—but the most awful taste came up my throat and into my mouth.

I lay on my bed in the living room, alternately coughing and burping and fighting to keep what little food I had eaten from coming back up. The pharmacist had told Dad that I would not, if I did have a tapeworm, get the full benefits of the medicine until about two weeks after I had finished the bottle. My pleurisy might start to improve within a few days and be gone altogether in two weeks.

But after days and days, none of my tapeworm-like symptoms lessened, and my pleurisy improved only slightly. So the doctors had me repeat the regimen—more money for more medicine, Jennie said—but with the same results, except that my cough came back with a vengeance.

After Jennie relayed this information to him, Dr. Barton called to say that, after conferring, he, Dr. Yap, Dr. Peddle and Dr. Hayward thought it was likely that my illnesses were idiopathic. That is, they were real but had no discoverable causes, meaning there were no cures for them and no way to relieve the symptoms other than to take over-the-counter medicines that would have only minimal effect. As with my arm, the pleurisy and stomach issues might or might not improve on their own.

The only things that could be fixed were my teeth. I would likely need to see an endodontist, to whom I would have to be referred by a dentist. In the meantime, the abscesses would recur, and I would need penicillin from time to time.

In the kitchen that night, after my brothers had gone to bed, Dad seemed almost gleeful that all these doctors of modern medicine had failed. He rhymed them off—McIntyre, Barton, Yap, Peddle, Hayward. They had failed, and now Wayne was worse off than he had been when he was rushed to McIntyre. He now had one useless arm, thanks to McIntyre, who had further distinguished himself by setting Child Welfare upon us when it was the doctors they should have been investigating.

Dad then wondered if there was such a thing as an idiopath. Osteopath. Homeopath. Idiopath: a specialist in diseases that had no discoverable causes and no discoverable cures. Dr. Stumped. Board-certified idiopaths, Drs. Stumped, Flummoxed and Mystified, third floor, turn right at the water cooler. Dad was not a reader, but he remembered quotations he had been made to memorize in school and wrung variations on them. Life is a tale told by an idiopath. TB or not TB, that is a question no idiopath can answer.

Jennie asked him if he was getting up and going into the bedroom so often because he had a flask hidden in there. Was he not aware that the upshot of the day's news was that nothing could be done for Wayne? Could he not put aside his inferiority complex long enough to realize that Wayne being no better off than before was not cause for gloating?

꩜

Idiopathy. To me, it was a word that meant I would *never* get better. It must have meant that to Jennie, too. Though she didn't let me see her crying, her eyes were red-rimmed and swollen for a week.

꩜

"Have those doctors all gone cracked?" Lucy said. "Idi—*what*?"

"Idiopathy."

"They have a name for a disease that doesn't exist?"

"It does exist and it's the same as some other people have but, in my case, they don't know *why* it's there. They said it has no discoverable cause."

"Well, that pretty much describes *you*. So you have pleurisy like other people have but theirs can be fixed and yours can't."

"I think so."

"Well. They only know what it does. Sure, *you* know that much. I know that much. I guess we're specialists. I never heard the like. What's the name of the tapeworm that you haven't got?"

I shrugged.

"You might as well get a second opinion from Larry Keiley down by Forest Pond. He calls him*self* an idiot, but he doesn't charge anyone anything for it. They know everything there is to know about your harmless heart murmur but nothing about what makes you sick. You poor soul."

❧

"Idiopathic," Mrs. Densmore said, writing it down. "I've never heard of that. I'll speak to someone about it. Dr. Barton, maybe, if he has the time."

"Yes, ma'am," Jennie said.

This was in the kitchen during Mrs. Densmore's fifth visit. Dad and I sat at the table with Jennie and her. If Mrs. Densmore asked to use the bathroom, Jennie was going to say that it was not working properly at the moment, but a plumber was coming by to fix it tomorrow. What she was going to say if Mrs. Densmore asked to use it on her next visit, she had no idea.

"So none of the medicines worked for you," Mrs. Densmore said to me, looking me over with dismay. I shook my head. I had idiopathic pleurisy. It sounded impressively grave.

"So the money you had coming must have arrived, did it, Mrs. Johnston? To pay for the medicine, I mean."

"Yes, ma'am," Jennie said. "It arrived from the mainland."

"So would you say that, at the moment, you're able to get along all right, money-wise?"

"Yes, ma'am."

"I've spoken to Father McGettigan, and he thinks that it will soon be a good time for Wayne to become an altar boy, if he still wants to."

"Yes, ma'am."

"Now that a lot of medical questions have been answered, I mean. Of course, some of the answers raised other questions, but still."

"Yes, ma'am."

"Even if there isn't very much Wayne can do because of his arm and his condition—just to be on the altar, sitting with the other boys, or even helping out in the sacristy before and after Mass, having some sort of social contact might do him a lot of good since he's not in school, don't you think?"

"Yes, ma'am. We need to get him a surplice and soutane, and a new pair of slippers like the other altar boys wear. We have the money, it's just that we might have to send away for a uniform his size. The Religious Supply Shop would have to, I mean. Wayne is very small. I haven't spoken to them, yet. I doubt they'll have his size."

The Religious Supply Shop. That didn't sound vague enough to be one of Jennie's stalling tactics.

twenty-four

One of our shortest winters ever gave way to an early spring. The snow melted. The ice on Forest Pond turned soft until it looked black and began to withdraw from the shore. Soon, there was nothing left of it but an island of slush that, impelled by wind and waves, drifted about the pond, getting smaller and smaller until, one morning, it was gone.

In March, Lucy had a relapse and Jennie went to stay with her again. Before she left, she told me that I would no longer be allowed to use Lucy's bathroom at night, because unannounced visits might interrupt her sleep. I asked Jennie when we'd have enough money for a plumber. She said she didn't know. Until we did, I would have to use what she called Ned's bathroom, but at least it was warmer outside now. Dad again took some vacation days so that I wouldn't be alone in the house during the week, nor the other boys on the weekends.

"Not a peep to Viola Densmore," Jennie said, though we hadn't seen Mrs. Densmore since Jennie had told her we were waiting for my altar boy uniform to arrive.

One Friday evening, Dad told Ken, Craig and Brian that he was taking me to a dental clinic that was open on Saturdays and that they would be going along for the ride. Craig said no, they were going fishing. Dad objected, saying that even if they went to a lake nearby, they would have to cross streams that were swollen by the early runoff, too deep and fast for them, especially Brian, to cross without his help.

Craig countered that they were going to fish a small river close to the house, one they wouldn't need to cross. But Dad insisted that they come with us—Jennie had insisted that they were not to be left on their own.

"No way am I getting in that car," Craig said. He was sure that Dad's real plan was to go to the Crystal, just as he had before when Lucy was sick, and leave us in the car to wait for God knows how long.

Dad swore he wouldn't go to the Crystal.

Ken and Brian could do as they liked, Craig said, but he was not getting in that car ever again unless Jennie was in it. Ken said he wasn't, either, and Brian said nothing, which Dad took to mean that he was siding with them.

Dad said that things had come to a fine pass when three boys would rise up in mutiny against their father. The three of them would hear about this from Jennie the next time they saw her, Dad threatened, but Craig said that she would side with them because she knew all his tricks as well as they did.

"Well that's a fine way to talk about your father," Dad said, and Craig said that, sooner or later, you had to draw the line, and this was where he was drawing his.

"Me, too," Ken said.

Brian looked panicked, as if it hadn't occurred to him that a refusal to get in the car tomorrow might escalate into a general drawing of lines.

"When do boys draw the lines about how far their fathers can or can't go?" Dad wanted to know. "Parents are the ones who draw the lines."

"Up to a point," Craig said. "Maybe there are some children who never have to draw the line on their father, but the drawing of this one is long overdue."

Dad told Craig to remember that just because they were too big for their britches didn't mean his children were too old to get their arse smacked.

Craig said that, while he was smacking one arse, the other two would be making a break for it. Brian started crying, but even I knew Dad was bluffing. He had never raised a hand to us, and his voice had that tone it took on when he knew he had lost an argument with Jennie. He went to his bedroom and slammed the door.

Early the next morning, my brothers snuck out of the house before Dad woke up. Craig stopped by my bed to grin at me. "Have fun waiting in the car," he said.

By the time Dad got up, I'd convinced myself that all that lay ahead of me was an afternoon of boredom while I waited alone in the car for Dad to emerge from the Crystal.

We left after lunch, Dad silent and brooding, puffing on a cigarette.

Soon after he turned right onto the Goulds Road, I saw the Crystal in the distance. We *had* to pass it to get to St. John's, but I closed my eyes and waited to hear the turn signal.

But we drove past. I told myself it was too soon to feel relieved, because he might drop into the Crystal on the way back, and there were other bars that he could go to, but I had the feeling that, if nothing else he'd said was true, he *was* taking me to a dentist.

As we drove, he told me he'd never been to a dentist in his life. Nor had the other boys or Jennie. I would be the first in the family. He smiled at me and I felt better.

After X-raying and examining my teeth, the dentist said that I would need quite a few root canals and other procedures before he could repair the broken teeth. When he told Dad how much my dental work would cost, Dad took my hand and walked me out of there.

On the way home, Dad said that, while there might not be much else to say in his defence, at least the dentist wasn't an idiopath. He knew what was wrong with me, and he knew how to fix it. He even knew *of* someone who could *pay* for it— Nelson Rockefeller, whose house would be our next stop. Dad said that the kind of needles dentists gave you were *supposed* to freeze your nerves, which probably meant that they would have no effect on mine. He said that he had never seen a priest with bad teeth, so maybe Father McGettigan was on to something about me going to the seminary. I would have to decide which I would find harder to give up, women or corn on the cob.

He was in such a good mood I thought a detour to the Crystal was certain. I didn't care. I could tell, just by the sound of it, how much a root canal would hurt and the toll it would take on what I had by way of a constitution. There was a cure for abscesses, even if it wasn't permanent. It wasn't hard to swallow penicillin.

Then, about a mile out of Kilbride, Dad suddenly floored the gas and tossed his cigarette out the window. Pushed back against the seat by the sudden surge of speed, I grabbed the armrest and looked at Dad, whose eyes were fixed on the rear-view mirror.

"What's wrong?"

When he ignored me, I looked behind us and saw that, despite the speed we were going, a station wagon was gaining on us.

"Jesus," Dad said, flooring it again. The back of the Dodge fishtailed. Now *we* were gaining on a light-blue Volkswagen Bug, which had turned onto the road in front of us and was moving very slowly. Dad pulled out to pass it just as the station wagon moved into the other lane, too.

The rear end of the Dodge hit the front end of the station wagon, which sent the Dodge careening into the Bug, bumping it onto the shoulder of the road and then into the ditch, where it skidded to a lurching stop.

Dad regained control of the Dodge. I looked about for the station wagon but couldn't see it. As we passed the stranded Bug, its driver, an old man, got out and shook his fist at us. The whole thing had taken a couple of deafening seconds—I had never heard a collision before.

"We hit two cars," I managed to say before I started coughing.

Again and again, Dad checked the rear-view. I turned around but still didn't see the station wagon.

"You should stop," I said, coughing after each word.

But he didn't slow down until we reached the outskirts of the Goulds, passing all the other cars on the road in front of us with just enough time to avoid oncoming traffic. All around us, drivers blew their horns.

Eyes still darting back and forth between the road and the rear-view, Dad slowed to the speed limit, sweat dripping from his chin, his face red. He turned onto Petty Harbour Road where, seeing no traffic in either direction, he again gunned it.

He pulled into our driveway without so much as touching the brakes, overshot his usual parking spot and drove straight past the house into the backyard. Had there been anyone round the corner, he'd have run them over. When he hit the brakes, the car kept going for thirty or forty feet, digging into the turf until at last it came to a hard stop that threw me against the dashboard, my left shoulder taking the brunt.

"Out, out, out," he said. "We have to get inside the house."

He easily beat me to the steps, which he ran up without a glance to see how I was doing. I had grabbed my bamboo cane from the back seat and done my best to keep up, but he was in the house by the time I reached the steps.

He'd left the door wide open. I found him in his bedroom, removing his clothes.

"Dad!" I said, but he gave no sign of having heard me. Once he was stripped down to his boxers, he got in bed, curled on his side and drew the blankets over himself so that only his hair showed.

"If the Mounties turn up," he said, "tell them I've been in bed, sick, all day. Go on. And don't call Jennie. Don't tell the boys."

As I turned to leave the room, I saw a half-full flask of Royal Reserve whisky on the floor beside his slacks. I picked it up, left the room and closed the door. I put the Royal Reserve on the counter in the kitchen, then went and knelt on the chesterfield and peered out. Across the road, all the curtains and blinds in Lucy and Ned's house were closed. I wondered if I should go over and get Jennie.

Surely Dad realized that, if the Mounties did turn up, they would see that the Dodge was newly dented and scraped. They would see the tire ruts in the grass and mud of the backyard. The drivers of the other two cars would have given the Mounties a description of his. Someone in all the cars we tore past on the way home to the Goulds might have recognized him or written down the number of his licence plate. I pictured him lying in that bed, eyes closed but wide awake, waiting for the sound of a siren. My heart pounded and my hands shook as I kept watch on the road, waiting for the police car's flashing lights.

Details of the pursuit, the two collisions and our zigzagging dash to Petty Harbour Road registered for the first time. There had been two men in the station wagon, though I hadn't been able to make out their faces. Their car was old, its fenders rusted, the strips of chrome that should have been fixed to the wooden panels on the side missing altogether.

Dad had never asked if I was all right. I told myself that he'd been lost in panic, concentrating on driving the car as he had likely never driven a car before. Why he'd had to, I couldn't guess. The bottle that had fallen out of his slacks meant that he'd been drinking before we left or even while I was being examined by the dentist, and I hadn't noticed.

Don't call Jennie. Don't tell the boys.

It might be possible to explain the damage to the Dodge. But did he really think it would be possible to explain what the car was doing in the backyard, up to its hubcaps in grass and mud? He'd be caught by someone, for sure. He'd never got away with anything, being so hapless at lies and alibis. It wouldn't take Jennie long to get the truth from him.

The second I thought of her, Jennie came out the front door of Lucy's house. Arms folded, she unhurriedly descended the steps and proceeded to the road, where she stopped to let a car that honked hello go by. Then, slowly, head down, as if she was pondering Lucy's health, she continued on her way, eyes fixed on the ground.

In this manner she walked down the driveway and disappeared round the corner of the house. As I got off the chesterfield, I heard her running up the steps. She flung open the door, which banged against the wall.

"Art," she shouted. She was soon in the living room, eyes darting about. "Jesus, Mary and Joseph," she said, and ran to me, crouching down and hugging me against her.

"Are you all right?" she said, patting me all over as if to make sure none of me was missing.

"Yeah," I said, starting to cry. "Dad drove really fast and hit some other cars."

"Merciful God!"

"He's okay, too," I said.

"What *happened*?"

"I'm not sure," I said. It was true. I wasn't sure in any but the most literal of ways.

"Where are your brothers?"

"They went fishing. They wouldn't go to the dentist with us because they thought Dad would duck into the Crystal."

"And where is *he*?"

"He got in bed."

She let go of me and made for the bedroom, reaching the door just as it opened. She went inside and the door closed behind her.

I was certain she would rip into him, but I didn't hear a sound. After about ten minutes of silence, I made out their voices, low but insistent, questioning, as if each of them was asking the other what their next step could possibly be, as if each of them was exasperated with the other's answers.

Then my brothers came storming up the back steps. I heard them kicking off their boots and throwing their fishing gear downstairs, talking excitedly. Craig reached the kitchen doorway when I did. Wide-eyed, mouth open in astonishment, he backed me into the hallway.

"WHAT HAPPENED TO THE FRIGGIN' CAR?" he roared, as if the answer could only be that it was all my fault.

Before I could say a word, my parents' bedroom door opened slightly. "The four of you, go to your room," Jennie said in a quiet tone that unsettled us all. "Shut the door and don't come out till I say so. Go on." She closed the door.

In the bunk room, Ken and Craig loomed over me and Brian climbed into his top bunk so that he could stare down at me, too.

"What happened?" Craig whispered, glancing at the door. He sounded as if he hated having to ask me, hated having missed something so *big*.

As I described the car chase, Craig said "Holy frig" every few seconds and looked at Ken, who was blank-faced and pale, with drops of sweat running from his temples and onto the sides of his face. His glasses were fogged up. I wondered from how far away they had seen that the car was in the back-yard, how far they had run to reach the house.

When I was done, Craig asked if I was sure that Dad had been trying to lose the station wagon and not just get to the Crystal as fast as he could. I told him how afraid and desperate Dad had looked, how he had hunched over the wheel and how he had seemed to forget entirely that I was in the car.

"Holy frig," Craig said again, then started to laugh as if I had recounted some adventure he wouldn't have thought me capable of having, or as if he was amused by how badly Dad had screwed up this time. "He never even stopped when the other car went into the ditch?"

I shook my head.

"Did he get hurt?" Ken said. "Did you?"

"My head hurts," I said.

Ken put a hand on my head and gingerly moved it about until I said, "Ow."

"There's a lump there," Ken said. "You must have banged your head pretty good on something. You didn't notice the headache until now?"

I shook my head. "My arm hurts, too," I said. "My bad one."

Ken took off my jacket and rolled up the sleeve of my shirt. "There's a bruise," he said, as Craig and Brian craned to see.

Craig said, "I thought you can't feel your arm."

"I can feel it when something hits the bone."

Craig tousled my hair as if my having been injured in a car accident was the first estimable accomplishment of my life.

Ken lay down on the bunk below Brian and put his hands behind his head and took off his glasses, still pale and sweaty.

"What do you think happened, Ken?" Craig said.

"Hit and run," Ken said. "That's pretty serious. And he was drinking."

Brian started to cry. Craig lay down on the other lower bunk, and I climbed up and sat beside Brian. Craig wondered if Dad would go to jail. Maybe someone had been badly hurt or even killed. Maybe Dad would go to jail for a long time on the mainland, where we couldn't afford to go to visit him. Maybe we'd never see him again, which would be fine with Craig and Dad, too, probably. Maybe we'd have to move to the mainland because of him. Everything would be different.

We waited for Jennie to emerge from their room, for the police to arrive, for the phone to ring. But nothing happened. Eventually Brian fell asleep. I climbed down and lay on the floor between the bottom bunks and wondered about Lucy and wished that I had asked Jennie how she was.

When we heard Dad and Jennie's door open, Craig and Ken were out of their bunks in a flash. Ken helped me to my feet as Brian climbed down. There was a knock on our door. When it opened, Jennie was there. Her eyes were red from crying, but she wasn't crying now.

She took hold of my good hand. "Come out to the kitchen, boys," she said. She gently pulled me from the room, and the others followed us to the kitchen. The flask of Royal Reserve that I'd put on the counter was no longer there.

After we had all sat down around the table, she said she had something to tell us. She lit a cigarette and was quiet for a while. Finally, Dad emerged from the bedroom, shirtless, and padded in his slippers to the kitchen. He sat in the last empty chair, the one between Jennie and me.

"Dad," Craig began, but Jennie shushed him. Dad merely stared at his hands, which lay on the table. He was clasping them so hard they were bloodless.

"No one says a word until I'm finished," Jennie said. "Something happened this afternoon." She looked about at my brothers and me as she spoke. There had been an accident, Jennie said, and she and Dad didn't know the names of the others involved, but Dad didn't think that anyone was hurt. We'd know why it had all happened when her story was done.

After leaving the dentist's office with Wayne, Dad had been chased by a car driven by two men to whom he owed a lot of money. She said the men in the station wagon were not the sort you could reason with, and there was no telling what they might have done, not just to Dad but to me. Immediately after the collisions, the station wagon had slowed down and turned off onto a side road, probably because the men thought the police were coming.

"Wayne said Dad drove like a maniac," Craig said. "He drove around the house like one. You can see the tracks."

"Your father did the best he could. Now, let me finish—your father only borrowed money from those men because of me."

"That's not friggin' true," Craig protested.

"It is," Jennie said, welling up. "He borrowed it to pay back eight hundred dollars I stole from Ned. During the winter, every time I went over there at night, I stole money from the stash that Ned keeps beneath the mattress of one of the beds. The one in the Shrine Room. Ned's never been to a bank. He's never accepted or written a cheque. Cash only. That's what he believes in. When I was ten, Lucy found out I knew where he kept his money. I found it by accident while I was making the beds, and she caught me counting it. She made me swear not to tell anyone and not to touch a penny of it, ever. She made me swear an oath to God with my hand on my heart.

"But when we ran out of money in January, I didn't know what else to do. I didn't even know if Ned still kept his money in the same place. But it turned out he did. Every night, while Ned was asleep, I stole his money. I figured he'd notice sooner or later, but I kept on stealing it anyway, fives and tens and twenties until one night Lucy caught me again.

"This time, she never said a word. She saw me from the doorway and went back to bed. The next day, I promised her I would pay back every cent—before she died, I meant, but I didn't say that. 'Pay it back when you can,' she said. 'Don't mention it to anyone, especially Ned.' But I couldn't stand the thought of her dying without me having paid it back. She might die thinking that I was still stealing from Ned. Or Ned might find out and she might die when they were on the outs.

"So I told your father. I told him that Ned would never lend money, never, not even if Lucy asked him to. He considers borrowing and stealing to be the same thing. She's the one who loaned us money over the years, without telling him. She loaned us *his* money. So, in a way, Lucy stole from Ned, too, but not like I did. Ned either didn't notice that money was missing or he did and never said anything to Lucy about it.

"I told your father how much trouble I was in. How much trouble *we* were in. I told him we had to do something. I knew about those men long before today."

Dad rose suddenly and hurried from the kitchen and into the bedroom, closing the door behind him, but not fast enough to drown out the sound of his sobs.

"I don't know how he found those men," Jennie said. "They don't advertise in the paper. He got hold of as much from them as he could, and I put the cash back beneath the mattress, but I still owe some to Ned. I just didn't know what to do. We didn't have a cent left. We already owed other people money. My family and your father's. I didn't know what to do. I almost got your father and Wayne and other people killed. I'm scared to death."

She dropped her forehead onto her arm on the table. Her shoulders shook. I was more frightened than I had been in the car. Jennie had stolen money from Ned. It didn't seem possible that Jennie had stolen anything from anyone. But she'd had to steal it, because Dad spent the rent, and because of me. My brothers looked terrified, too. It seemed to me that all order had been overthrown and could never be restored, because of Dad and me. Craig put his hand on Jennie's arm. I put mine on her back. Brian put his next to mine. Ken put his forehead on the top of Jennie's head and his arms around all of us.

The police didn't come. The phone didn't ring.

twenty-five

One day, after Jennie had come home to take a break—
Dot Chafe was with Lucy—she told me there were after-
noons when Lucy was feeling well enough for a visit from me.
She reminded me not to say a word about Ned's money.

I went over there and found Lucy in the Shrine Room again,
in the single bed, beside which Jennie had set a kitchen chair
for me. Lucy looked much better than she had the day of her
false alarm. She sat propped up by pillows, her arms resting on
the blankets, a set of new ruby-red prayer beads in her hands.

She was clear-headed most of the time, despite the painkill-
ers she was on, though every so often she nodded off, and she
meandered as she spoke, leaving one topic only to return to it.

"Have you got another miracle left in you for Lucy?" she
asked me.

When I didn't answer, she appraised the Baby Jesus.

"It looks odd, doesn't it, a baby with a crown on its head. I wonder what baby food was like back then. How long would a crown stay on the head of an ordinary baby? Not long without a chinstrap. But I suppose the Baby Jesus is not like other babies. He could balance anything on his head, never mind a crown. Still, maybe the halo holds it in place. I've never met a youngster who deserved a halo. Or *anyone* who did, have you?"

She said that when she looked at her own boys when they were two years old, a halo was not what came to mind.

"I don't want a wake. I'll be in no position to prevent one, so Ned better remember that I said I didn't want one. *You* remember. This house has already had one wake too many. Three days and nights with Leonard laid out in the living room. Just before Christmas.

"It's hard to sleep when there's a casket in the house. I don't mean because of ghosts or anything like that, but that's what the youngsters were afraid of. I swear they were never the same. Jennie wasn't. It was so sad to see Leonard all dressed up. We had never spent as much money on clothes for him when he was alive.

"I never saw the point of a wake. No one who was alive could stand to be stared at and talked about so much. I know more than one person who'll get their licks in when I'm in no condition to talk back, people who'd run now if I said boo. No wake, no. There'd be no one here but Ned at night, and me laid out in some other room. He'd think about Leonard. He'd think about things that he forgot. Why should he put himself through that?

"I'll miss Ned. And you. I'll miss my children. But they have their wives and husbands and their own children. Leonard has no one."

It was as if Leonard had hold of her and Ned and was slowly but surely tugging them to the other side.

She looked at me, then, and said I better be ready—that body of mine might still have things to throw at me, even though it had already thrown more at me than God had thrown at Job.

"Whatever happens to you, make sure you don't clam up like Ned because of it. Don't wallow in misery. No one's ever had a stretch of happiness so long that they got fed up with it.

"It's been touch and go with you since you fizzled out when you were one. Once you've been close to the other side, it's hard to feel at home in this one. That's why I'm back in this bed. It was touch and go with me, too, before you lit the candle and said your prayer that day, but not for nearly as long as it has been with you.

"Even after I was back on my feet, I knew it wouldn't last. You may be young, but most of you is still back there where you were when you first got sick—ready to cross over. You have to try really hard to resist the other side, or else you'll wind up there before your time." She paused. "No one would ever mistake this for a pep talk, would they?"

It occurred to me that Leonard hadn't lingered long enough for people to get tired of him being sick.

"Until you came along, I'd never known people to look at a child and say that he'd seen better days. Still, unless God takes you before your next birthday, you won't be seven forever.

Things change. You will. It might not seem like that to you right now, but it's true.

"You read more books in a week than anyone I know has read in their entire life. I never saw the point of books, but there might be one. You better hope there is. You have a lot of time invested in them that you won't get back.

"I worry a bit about Ned. The man has cobwebs on his vocal cords. Five minutes in the confession box on Saturday. That's more talking than he does all week, unless you count the rosary.

"Mind you, he might not even say a word in there. The priest might have to guess his sins. 'Am I getting warm, Ned? One knock for no, two for yes.' We're a perfect match, a woman who doesn't like to be interrupted and a man who never says a word. Still, it would be nice to know if he listens to me. I've never seen him taking notes.

"You're stronger than people think you are. You rarely complain, which is just as well, because complaining takes energy and you have none to spare. You were put on earth for a reason, although it wouldn't surprise me if God himself can't remember what it is. There's nothing wrong with getting off to a bad start—it might save you a lot of disappointment, or you'll give someone, your mother maybe, a pleasant surprise by making something of yourself. There's nothing wrong with being a complete flop right from the start. It's better than getting everyone's hopes up for nothing. That's what most people do before they fizzle out."

"How long was Leonard sick?"

"A few months. *Really* sick for a couple of weeks. He had to have his own room. Me and two of my sisters took turns staying with him. He couldn't be alone. We were worried that the rest of the youngsters would catch it, but they never did."

"Was he scared?"

"He was too sick, too tired, to be scared. Were you scared the night they buried you in ice?"

"No."

"Leonard made his first confession and took his First Holy Communion a month before he died. Right here in this house, because he was too weak to go to church. He was such a sweet boy, but he wasn't strong like you. When the doctor said tuberculosis, I knew he never had a chance.

"You have it in your head that you're like Leonard. That might be my fault. You're nothing like him. You remind Ned of Leonard, but everything reminds Ned of Leonard. Don't you worry about me. I can take care of myself."

If there was nothing to be afraid of in heaven, I asked her, why did it matter that she needed to be able to take care of herself?

"It takes a while to get the hang of a new place. You should know that, after the number of times you've moved. There are people who have been in heaven a long time. It might not be easy to fit in with people who've been there a thousand years. I bet that people were a lot different a thousand years ago. I know there were kings and queens all over the place. What will they make of me? I'm sure I'll be put in my place more than once. I can be a bit of an upstart. I might rub someone the wrong way. I'm not used to being new in a place, because

I've never been anywhere but the Goulds. I can't even stand St. John's. People walk right past you without even saying hello. And there's a lot more people in heaven than there are in St. John's. They might be a bit uppity."

She said that, over the years, whenever one of her relatives was close to death, she thought about asking them to look in on Leonard until she got to heaven, but she could never find the right moment to ask a favour from someone who was dying.

She said that going to heaven might be like going to sleep in one place and waking up in another. That had happened to her once. When she was a child, she was outside, and she fell and hit her head on something. When she woke up, she was in bed in the house. There was nothing in between. No dreams. No sounds. There wasn't even darkness.

She said, "You don't remember passing out, you remember waking up, but what about if you don't wake up?"

She was sure she would wake up tomorrow, but she couldn't help thinking she might not. She couldn't help being a bit scared. But maybe going to heaven wasn't like that. Maybe you did see things along the way. The moon, the sun, the stars. Maybe you could feel the wind like you did in the back of a truck. Maybe you could hear it. But maybe you were wide awake and everything was dark and you couldn't hear a sound. It might be like that for a long time because heaven was so far away.

She said she didn't talk about such things with Father McGettigan, or with Ned, or with anyone but me, which wasn't right because I wasn't old enough—maybe no one was. I might think bad things because of her or have bad dreams if

I managed to stay asleep long enough to have a dream of any kind. But it was too late to worry about that now. She was sorry. I should tell God it was Lucy's fault if I thought bad things or had bad dreams.

"I might be used to heaven by the time you get there. The people there might be used to me. When you get there, ask around for me, Lucy Everard. There'll be more than one Lucy. Ask around for us, Lucy and Leonard Everard. And maybe Ned by then."

I knew she didn't expect me to outlive Ned. She didn't expect me to outlive anyone, except her. Maybe no one did. Maybe Dad and Jennie were keeping things from me and from my brothers, or maybe Jennie had sworn my brothers to secrecy. Maybe the doctors knew things that Dad and Jennie and even Mrs. Densmore didn't know. As usual, everything was maybe and nothing was for sure.

At Lucy's instruction, I lit the votive candle. I stood the matchbox on its side and, with the fingers of the same hand, scraped the match along the rough surface.

"That's a good trick," Lucy said.

I knelt in front of Mary and the Baby Jesus when Lucy told me to, and we went on talking until she said it was time to say a prayer. As always, I was supposed to close my eyes but didn't. Instead, I watched her, her eyes shut, her lips moving as if she was silently reciting something she had memorized.

"I'll be fine," she said, but the words came out beneath her breath, lower than a whisper. "Give me a hug, just in case."

I hugged her with my one good arm, pressing my cheek against her hair.

twenty-six

A few days later, about nine in the evening, the telephone rang. Dad answered. I knew it was Jennie calling by the look on his face. After a few seconds, he went out into the porch and closed the door. I knew what that meant, and I could tell by the looks on my brothers' faces that they knew, too.

Before he came back, cars began to arrive at Ned and Lucy's, though, as Lucy herself had predicted, not nearly as many as on the day she had sent for me.

This time it was just her children, caught by surprise. She had died in her sleep when not even Jennie had been in the room. After twenty minutes or so, Dad came back from the porch and turned off the TV.

"Boys," he said. He didn't say anything else. He made his way around the house, closing the blinds, drawing the curtains. He came back to the living room, sat on the chesterfield and lit a cigarette. He said that Jennie and some of the others were going to keep Ned company for the next few days. My brothers would be staying home from school. The five of us, the men of the house, would be holding down the fort.

He said that he had promised Jennie that he wouldn't take a drink, and he wouldn't. We might not believe him, but we'd see.

He sounded angry as he told us it was going to be hard on Jennie for a while and she was counting on us. We had to take care of each other because Jennie had too much on her plate right now. She had enough to worry about without worrying about us. He sounded even angrier, as if we had already let our mother down, already misbehaved.

I guessed that he had offered to go over or, more likely, had asked her if she wanted him to. That was how he would have put it. *Do you want me to come over?* And she had said no because she knew he didn't really want to. Maybe even because she didn't want him to. Jennie would be fine because John was there, the brother she was closest to.

Dad was angry with himself and her, angry enough to make a promise that he didn't have to make and wouldn't keep. He *would* take a drink, but not where we could see him. He would drink straight from the bottle when we weren't looking.

He didn't once mention Lucy's name. When he was finished talking, he went to the bedroom and closed the door.

"Come in with us," Craig said to me.

I went with them to the bunk room for a while, but I started to cough, so I went back to the living room and parted the curtains and peered out through the blinds. Ned and Lucy's was lit up, every room, though all the curtains were drawn. I saw shadows moving back and forth, as if everyone was standing up, trying to look as though they were pitching in, though there wasn't much to do. Lucy was in the Shrine Room with Mary and the Baby Jesus and the people who had come to say goodbye. But she was in heaven, too.

Give me a hug, just in case.

She said that the last time I went to see her. She'd known. *I* should have known. But I was glad we hadn't had to say goodbye. I was glad that I hadn't known that our last meeting would *be* the last. Then I remembered that, when we knelt before the Shrine after Craig fought with the foster boy, Lucy had said to me: "Let's say our prayer . . . I'll say one for you and you say one for me, all right?" She had prayed for me— for exactly what, I didn't know, though I suspected that she'd prayed that my illnesses would go away. They hadn't. But I hadn't prayed for her, and she had died. How many times she had prayed for me I would never know, but not even on the day of her false alarm had I prayed for her. I wondered whether, if I had prayed even once that her illness would go away, it would have.

I went out to the back porch, where I kept my bamboo cane, stood the cane at an angle against the wall and tried to break it with my foot, but the bamboo was so stringy it only cracked lengthwise into half a dozen strands.

I took it into the kitchen and snapped it over and over like a whip, but it still wouldn't break. Fed up with my utter uselessness, I tossed the cane back into the porch and closed the door.

I lay on my bed in the living room and repeatedly punched my left arm with my right fist, feeling next to nothing most of the time, otherwise a kind of faint electric shock. I sawed the back of my good hand with the edges of my broken teeth, which were now so dulled they didn't even break the skin but only left a few red lines.

I struck my chest with my fist in the place I imagined my murmuring heart to be, but it went on beating normally.

Not long ago, I had happened upon one of the places that Dad hid flasks of Royal Reserve, between a stack of towels in the hall closet. I got off the bed and looked in the closet, finding a flask with about an inch of whisky left.

I took it back to my bed, sat down, unscrewed the top and took a swallow, certain it would set off a coughing fit like no other I had ever had. It scorched my mouth and throat and burned all the way to my stomach, but there the burning turned to a warm, pleasant glow.

I took another swallow that had the same effect. How strange it would be if the only tonic for my cough and my stomach's tendency to reject most foods and liquids turned out to be my dad's forbidden booze.

I finished the bottle. I thought of how sad and guilty Dad looked when he was drinking. I felt happy, elated, buoyant. I replaced the top, put the empty bottle beneath my pillow and lay down.

I thought of Leonard, wandering around heaven by himself, homesick and lonely and down in the dumps until Lucy found him and told him who she was, for though Leonard was still seven, Lucy had aged so much he wouldn't recognize her.

I imagined Leonard going over to Lucy's place in heaven every day to play cards with her and kneel before the Shrine and drink chocolate Quik, Leonard taking my place in heaven as I had taken his on earth.

What would Lucy tell Leonard about me? They'd have a good laugh, I figured, but they wouldn't be mean. "You've never met a stranger youngster. Everything there was to catch, he caught it. He caught diseases we didn't even have in Newfoundland. You didn't need an X-ray to see his insides, just a flashlight. He knocked himself out cold on the bathroom sink one night. He brought enough food back up to feed Biafra. His arm was so skinny, a doctor broke it with a booster shot. He had a smoker's cough even though he never smoked. He was afraid to go to sleep in case he missed something."

I woke in the dark, my body pulsing with pain from the top of my head to the soles of my feet, keeping perfect time with my heart, which was going like mad. I swung my feet onto the floor and, using my good arm, managed to sit up. I stood—or thought I did. I hadn't moved at all. I tried again and wound up on the floor, lying on my good side. After several tries, I managed to rock myself into a crawling position, balanced on my knees and my one good hand.

I scuffed and lurched along the floor, bound for the toilet that had not been used in months, the toilet that must not be flushed, the toilet cover that must not be raised no matter what—bound for it because I assumed that the culmination of this pain would be a bout of sick that would outdo the one that caused the fever that had taken all the ice of Petty Harbour Road to bring down by three degrees.

I was just a few feet from the bathroom when the bunk room door swung wide. I saw a pair of feet in slippers but couldn't bear to raise my head enough to see another inch.

"Holy frig," said a voice that I assumed belonged to the person whose feet I was staring at. "*Ken*, there's something wrong with Wayne," the voice said, its owner now kneeling beside me and massaging my neck with one hand. "He smells like *Dad*," the voice whispered.

I felt several hands drag me into the bunk room on my stomach. Then I was hoisted into one of the lower bunks.

"Holy frig, he's *drunk*," Craig said. "How did he get drunk?"

"Maybe he licked a beer bottle cap. You're all right, Wayne, just lie down."

That was Ken.

Craig laughed.

"Don't wake up Dad," Ken said to him. Then to me, "Just lie back, Wayne. Stop trying to get off the bed."

Ken laughed a little, too.

"Will you give me a hand with him, Craig?"

"He's *plastered*," Craig said. He tousled my hair.

Hours later. The pulsing pain let up as my heart slowed down. I was still drunk. Drunk. Craig didn't know what that was like. He didn't know what being me was like. He never had and never would.

"Lucy is with Leonard, now," said a voice that I was fairly

certain was my own. Leonard had been Lucy's all along. Lucy's boy.

I fell asleep, crying, in Craig's arms.

Craig was asleep in his bunk when I woke up. I didn't feel too bad, but I knew that I would start to cough if I stayed in bed, so I got up. I crept out of the room. Across the way, the house was dark.

twenty-seven

There was no wake, as Lucy had asked, and that was fine with me. I didn't want to see her in a casket. I didn't want Lucy to be laid out for three days in that house, as she told me Leonard had been. I didn't want to be led to the living room by Jennie and have to kneel with her while she held my hand to keep me from losing my balance and tipping over sideways like a statue. I didn't want to walk among the same grown-ups I had walked among the day Lucy had her false alarm, Jennie's boy dressed to the nines as if nice clothes could disguise the fact that I looked as though I would be the next to go.

There was a funeral Mass, but I didn't go to it. I told Jennie that I knew there was no chance I would be able to get through it without a coughing fit that would require me to be led, or carried, from the church. I was telling the truth, but I also didn't want to put in a final appearance as Lucy's boy and give in to everyone's expectation that I would bawl my eyes out.

I spent the day of the funeral at home with Dad, who'd volunteered to mind me. As he sipped beer in silence at the kitchen table, I told him I had to go across the road to use the bathroom. At Ned and Lucy's, I took a pill bottle from the medicine cabinet. In the bottle, which I had put there weeks ago, was the sixty-five cents I had stolen from Dad the day he left us in the car at the Crystal.

I went back home. Not much later, Dad said he hadn't had much sleep the night before and was going to take a nap. I waited until I thought it was safe, crept into the bedroom and put the sixty-five cents in the pocket of Dad's slacks which, as always, he had thrown on the floor. Then I crept out of the room and eased the door shut.

In the evenings, I saw the blue flicker of the television set in the dark front room across the road. Ned watching TV.

"Poor soul," Jennie would say and, every so often, she crossed the road to visit him. She came back after ten or fifteen minutes, which was as long as she could stand to go without a cigarette while staying silent in her father's company. She always waited until she was back at our house to light one up.

Jennie and I were allowed to use Lucy's bathroom again. At first, I waited until late to cross the road and crept inside, more quietly than I used to. Even with Jennie's help, Ned didn't keep things as clean as Lucy had. It was as if he was waiting for the house to clean itself.

Jennie put out food for Murchie from Lucy's dwindling supply and filled his water dish and cleaned his cat box. I asked her what would become of Murchie. Could we have him? She said she didn't know what would happen to Murchie, but he would not be coming to live with us. Ned hadn't mentioned him, and she hadn't asked Ned about him, but she knew she would have to eventually.

The house smelled so much of Murchie and his food that, on more than one night when I went over there long after the TV had been turned off, I went to the kitchen and peered beneath the daybed. Murchie wasn't there.

Sometimes, I stood in the hallway like an intruder who meant to do Ned harm. Once, overcome by a longing to see the Shrine Room again, to see the bed in which Lucy had died, the mattress beneath which Ned kept his money, perhaps to look at the money itself, I went down the hall.

The door was closed, but I found that it was unlocked when I tried the knob. I eased it open and there, in the single bed, sound asleep and snoring, was Ned. From the door, I could just make out the statue of the Blessed Virgin and the Baby Jesus in the corner. The votive candle was lit, but there was not much of it left. He must have lit it when he went to bed. The flame flickered as it always did, as if there was a draft, though I'd never felt one and didn't now.

I wondered if Ned had stopped sleeping in his and Lucy's bed for good or only for a while—because he missed Lucy, because, without her, it was a marriage bed no more, because he couldn't bear the emptiness of it, the unused half, the oddness of lying on whichever side was his while the other one was empty. Or had he noticed that money was missing from beneath the Shrine Room bed and told Lucy about it? Had he got the truth from her and confronted Jennie? He might have come to some sort of arrangement with her and Dad, a forgiveness of the loan, a general forgiveness. Or had he, as Jennie had feared, had a falling out with both her and Lucy?

I made my way on tiptoe to the Shrine. I saw the photographs, but the light was so dim I couldn't make out which one was that of Ned and Leonard in the hayfield.

Perhaps it was knowing it was there but not being able to make it out that unlocked its meaning: in that sun-drenched hayfield, I'd noticed before that Ned was smiling but Leonard was not. When had I ever seen Ned smile?

In the photograph, Ned is smiling because he knows, he *knows,* what Leonard doesn't and must never know.

I wondered if, at some point near the end of my life, someone would smile for me like that.

I began going over there to use the bathroom when Ned was still up.

When I opened the side door, then the inner door to the hallway, he didn't say a word. Nor did I.

One night, around ten, I crossed the road to his house, not to use the bathroom but to see if I could work up the nerve to go down the hallway to the living room, where he sat watching TV—what I would do then, what he would do, I wasn't sure.

I let myself in as usual but turned right instead of left and slowly made my way down the hall, half expecting Ned to ask me what I wanted or tell me to leave.

When I stopped in the doorway of the living room, he kept his eyes on the television screen. He was sitting on the far end of the chesterfield, close to the window, his hands in his lap, his feet crossed on the floor.

As my eyes adjusted to the light, I made out Murchie, sitting in an armchair across the room from Ned, his yellow eyes, though fixed on me, sleepily opening and closing.

"Hi, Murchie," I said.

The cat roused himself just enough to more or less roll from the chair. He landed on his feet, padded past me and down the hallway to the kitchen door, where he turned, his body and, finally, his tail slowly disappearing.

I sat at the other end of the chesterfield from Ned and looked at the screen. The sound was lower than I was used to. I don't remember what we watched, only that we sat like that in silence for, perhaps, twenty minutes. My heart fluttered, pounded, fluttered again.

I felt a cough coming on and was about to get up and make a quick exit when, without turning to look at me, Ned said, "Did you see the mist on the pond this morning, Wayne?"

"Yeah," I said.

He nodded.

"Lucy liked the mist," he said.

afterword

We stayed three more months in that house, then moved to another in the Goulds, in which the first girl of the family, Cynthia, was born. We kept moving until we settled down in a brand-new house on the very site of the half house, which had been torn down after being condemned.

"I knew," Jennie said. "I knew this was as far as I would get."

Time would prove her wrong.

About six months after Lucy died, something inside me began to tilt toward life. Over the next few years, my body changed. By ten, I was eating voraciously and keeping everything down, though I didn't gain an ounce until I began, at twelve, to grow taller.

I grew seven inches in one year, five inches the next, four the year after that. I'm now six two, weirdly taller than the rest of my family.

I became an eclectic athlete, somewhat adept at every sport I tried, taking joy in figuring out the something-more-than-meets-the-eye in every one of them, and in unfettered self-propulsion. I probably wouldn't appreciate having a body that can do so much if I hadn't once had one that could do next to nothing.

When I was thirty, I went to a dentist for the second time in my life. That was many root canals ago. It is still my habit to hide my teeth by never smiling with anything except my eyes.

My nervous cough became less and less frequent until it no longer acted up. The pleurisy, too.

By the time I was fourteen, my left arm had completely healed and I went back to being left-handed, though I am more or less ambidextrous when I want to be.

The one part of my "condition" that did not improve to everyone's liking, though it has never bothered me very much, was my insomnia. Robert Frost wrote that he was "one acquainted with the night." So am I. I write at night, sleep for a couple of hours, and otherwise live by day. I do not have the gift of sleep. People tell me that I don't know what I'm missing. They're right, but so am I when I say the same of them.

For years, many people, including me, assumed I would be a priest. As the time drew near for me to enter the seminary, I realized I had no interest in the priesthood because I had no idea what it was. I decided to become a doctor. I completed pre-med and again changed my mind. I became a serial quitter until I happened upon a job as a newspaper reporter when I was twenty-one. There is, as I've often been told, a book in that.

I owe an unrepayable debt to the dozens of people who, without knowing they were doing so, loaned their memories to the writing of *this* book, especially Lucy, Jennie, my father and brothers and sisters, though there are an innumerable host of others, and also to the dozens and dozens whom I think of as my "other" family at Penguin Random House Canada.

I have come to believe that, unlike my childhood illnesses, life is not idiopathic. It has a discoverable cause and, whatever its duration, many purposes.

WAYNE JOHNSTON was born and raised in Goulds, Newfoundland. Widely acclaimed for his magical weaving of fact and fiction, his masterful plotting and his gift for both description and character, his #1 nationally bestselling novels include *First Snow, Last Light*, *The Custodian of Paradise*, *The Navigator of New York* and *The Colony of Unrequited Dreams*. *Baltimore's Mansion*, a memoir about his father and grandfather, won the inaugural Charles Taylor Prize for literary non-fiction. *The Colony of Unrequited Dreams*, published in 1998, was nominated for sixteen national and international awards including the Scotiabank Giller Prize and the Governor General's Literary Award for Fiction, and was a Canada Reads finalist defended by Justin Trudeau. A theatrical adaptation of the novel recently toured Canada. His most recent novel is *The Mystery of Right and Wrong*.